# *18*

| | | |
|---|---|---|
| *Josefina Ayerza* | To resume again… | 2 |
| *Jacques-Alain Miller* | Lacanian Biology | 6 |
| *Richard Klein* | Gender and Sexuation | 30 |
| *Thomas Svolos* | The Great Divide | 42 |
| *Gerard Wajcman* | The Absence of the 20th Century | 60 |
| *Slavoj Zizek* | *Il n'y a pas de rapport religieux* | 80 |
| *JA* | Rosemarie Trockel | 106 |
| | Intercepts | 110 |
| *Richard Klein* | New & Noteworthy Books | 124 |

JUERGEN TELLER's work courtesy Lehmann Maupin Gallery, NY. MARTÍN LARRALDE's work courtesy Annina Nosei Gallery, NY. JITKA HANZLOVÁ's work courtesy of Klemens Gasser & Tanya Grunert, Inc., NY. RINEKE DIJKSTRA's work courtesy Marian Goodman Gallery, NY. ROSEMARIE TROCKEL's work courtesy The Drawing Center, NY. PIA STADTBÄUMER's work courtesy Sean Kelly Gallery, NY. DAMIEN HIRST's work courtesy Gagosian Gallery, NY.

JACQUES-ALAIN MILLER is a practicing analyst who teaches Psychoanalysis at Paris VIII. He is Editor-in-Chief of the journal *Ornicar?* and sole editor of Jacques Lacan's Seminars and writings.

RICHARD KLEIN is GP—primary care physician—in Oxford, UK, till 1991. He participates in the Freudian Field since 1985, he is a member of the European School of Psychoanalysis, a member of the WAP (AMP), and a psychoanalyst in private practice, London.

THOMAS SVOLOS is a psychoanalyst-in-training at the Creighton-Nebraska Psychiatry Residency Training Program in Omaha, NE. He obtained his MD from the University of California, San Francisco, and his BA from Duke University.

GÉRARD WAJCMAN is a French psychoanalyst, member of L'École de la Cause, Paris. He wrote *L'objet du siècle* (Paris: Verdier, 1998). *L'invention du caché* is forthcoming from the same publisher.

SLAVOJ ZIZEK is the author of several works on philosophy, psychoanalysis, and popular culture. His most recent books include *Did Somebody Say Totalitarianism? Four Interventions in the (Mis)Use of a Notion* and *The Fragile Absolute Or, Why the Christian Legacy is Worth Fighting For*.

JOSEFINA AYERZA is a writer and practicing psychoanalyst in New York City. She writes regularly for *Flash Art*.

Cover: JUERGEN TELLER
*Miss Guatemala*, C-print
on aluminum, 2000
*Miss Sweden*, C-print
on aluminum, 2000
Courtesy of Lehmann Maupin Gallery, NYC

# To resume again...

How is it that Miss Sweden on the cover of *lacanian ink* 18, and Ms. Guatemala on the back cover spell out the non-rapport?

 Miss Sweden and Miss Guatemala embody the line of sight that defines desire as positioning on behalf of the place that invests them. The line of sight focuses on an image that is a mystery, thus an obscure object, still set out to conquer a universal stance. Whether you like her or not Miss Universe will hold the scepter which represents the desire of all men. Yet after a year a new flower will bloom, rekindling the desire of all men, for a whole new year. And this is the fate of the contemporary Aphrodite. Will she ever be the One?

 Between man and woman there is no instinctual rapport because sexuality is marked by the signifier. Thus an Other sits between them. And there is no reciprocity because the Other—the symbolic order—is asymmetric: there is no signifier for the woman...only one signifier, the phallus, rules over the rapport of the sexes. "The sexual rapport cannot be written."

 For Lacan "The most naked rivalry between men and woman is eternal." Love then is the illusion for the absence of harmonic rapport between the sexes. Man does not enjoy the body of the woman, only the body part—sexual drives go solely towards the partial object. With Jacques-Alain Miller, "body parts can certainly be represented, beside with other natural elements, yet they account for signifiers. They are imaginary signifiers whose matter is taken from the image. When we say 'the living body,' we leave aside both the symbolized body and the body image. The body affected by *jouissance* is neither imaginary nor symbolic, but a living one." Life is a condition of *jouissance*. "Life overflows the body. What obliges you to attest there isn't *jouissance* unless life appears under the form of a living body."

Richard Klein discusses gender, "The fundamental trauma is no longer castration which the phallus includes. Traumatic is the sexual non-rapport in that the sexual relation is a hole in the real. It is *troumatique*. Nothing like a hole to indicate that something that does not exist can still operate."

With Svolos the non-rapport issue addresses asymmetry in the direction of the cure—when it comes to psychosis, the cure should take on the use of pills, on the use of words?

In "The Absence of the 20th Century," the non-rapport already insinuated in the title, Gérard Wajcman discusses the art of Jochen Gerz. "After all, Adorno conceivably fell shy when he declared the impossibility of poetry in the aftermath of Auschwitz (or, as I suggested in the beginning, it may be peremptory to dissociate art and poetry in this respect)."

As something tied to the real, sex opposes sense, to the point, with Slavoj Zizek, where woman is one of the names of God—there is no sexual rapport, there is no religious rapport. In his *Il n'y a pas de rapport sexuel*, "the story of (Adam's) Fall is evidently the story of how the human animal contracted the excess of Life which makes him/her human—'Paradise' is the name for the life delivered of the burden of this disturbing excess."

JA

Martin Larralde, *Untitled*, oil on linen, 2000

# Lacanian Biology and the Event of the Body*

JACQUES-ALAIN MILLER
translated by BARBARA P. FULKS

I. EXAMINING THE ALGORITHMS OF LIFE
THE CONCEPT OF LIFE

Finding myself again with the work of Freud, Lacan, and the practice of psychoanalysis, I see that I have carefully circumvented an explanation of the coordinates of the concept of life. I must say that this is an eminently problematic concept, and one of which Lacan said, in his 1955 Seminar: "The phenomenon of life remains in its essence completely impenetrable. It continues to escape us no matter what we do." One might ask if Lacan knew at that time of the decisive step of Watson and Crick's truly epochal discovery of the structure of DNA. Their very brief initial article, "Molecular Structure of Nucleic Acids," appeared in the journal *Nature* in 1953 and inaugurated the triumphal years of genetics. We are today at the dawn of the century which will see the sensational practical consequences of this step.

Is the phenomenon of life therefore penetrable after the discovery of this structure? Quite the contrary. In 1970, one of the crafters of the triumphs of molecular genetics, François Jacob, could say, in his book *The Logic of Life*: "We do not question life any more in the laboratory; we no longer try to encompass its contours. We only try to analyze living systems."[1] It is a fact that, when we

* *L'orientation lacanienne*, Paris, Spring 1999.

analyze the living being, not in its superb stature—its unity evident at the macroscopic level—but rather at the level of the molecule, the processes in play highlight the physics and the chemistry involved but do not at all distinguish themselves from the processes which unfold in inanimate matter, in inert systems.

Lacan's statement, then, is perfectly true in spite of the progress of molecular biology. As François Jacob said, the decline of the concept of life does not date from the middle of this century, but from the advent of thermodynamics: "The operational value of the concept of life had to decline after the birth of thermodynamics."

This perspective is perfectly coherent with that explained by Lacan in the beginning chapters of his Seminar *The Ego*,[2] where he pointed out that Freudian biology is first of all an energetics. This is the route he would take up, in his own way, as he resumes that year and afterwards the lessons of *Beyond the Pleasure Principle*. Because Freudian biology is first of all an energetics, Lacan allows himself to say that Freudian biology is not a biology. This is so if we understand by biology a discipline which has life as its object, but it is certainly less correct now that we have in some way a biology without life, a biology which has as its object—this is one of Jacob's expressions, but it could just as well be Lacan's—"the algorithms of the living world." This expression reveals the notion of a procedure, marked by a certain vagueness, central to biology. In this context Lacan formulated in *Encore* (1972)[3] what could pass for an analytic concept of life which seems to define life as *jouissance*: "We don't know what it means to be alive except for the following fact, that a body is something that enjoys itself (*cela se jouit*)." It is that a definition of life? It is rather the opposite. We do not know what life is. We only know that there is no *jouissance* without life. And why not formulate the principle in this way: life is the condition of *jouissance*. But that is not all. It is precisely a matter of life under the form of the body. *Jouissance* is unthinkable without the living body, itself the condition of *jouissance*. This point of departure justifies reopening the biology dossier.

## 1. LIFE AND THE ONE OF THE BODY

In our discipline, which is clinical, life presents itself to us in the form of the individual body, and we can remain there. We are even obliged to remain there.

It is there that one can make a distinction between life and body, as in the expression "living body." Life is not reduced to body in its beautiful and evident unity. There is evidence of the individual body, of the body as One, which is a sign of the imaginary order.

Let us take care to be a little flexible in questioning the status of the individual in regard to life, and especially the status of this One who appears in some way natural. All of Lacan's Seminar called *Encore* is pervaded by this insistent interrogation: must we think that the One comes to us from the pretext of this imaginary evidence of the unity of the body? What is the value of the other position, the thesis that the One comes to us from the signifier and not from the One of the body? Lacan did a lot to test this evidence. In particular he wrote a sentence about zoology which merits attention and development. "Zoology can proceed from the pretense of the individual to make being (*être*) of life (*vivant*), but the individual is diminished by this discipline to the level of a polypary."

When we are dealing with animal, with the living (*vivant*), it is the individual, the body-one. We can say that the living being is realized in an individual. But what can we then make of the polyps, the polyparies that inspired our 18th century materialists— Trembley's famous polypary which was conceived as simultaneously mineral, vegetable and animal? What to make of the colony of coral in which corporeal individuality becomes eminently problematic? We find ourselves before a sort of collective semi-individualized being which seems to be there in order to fill the gaps in the chain of beings.

### D'ALEMBERT'S DREAM

A whole line of thought has been devoted to the notion that everything is continuous in matter, leading us from the inanimate to the living without addressing the problem of continuity. Diderot's *d'Alembert's Dream* was written to show at what point life exceeds the poor One of body and appears to the contrary like an extraordinary drive of proliferation. D'Alembert's dream, properly stated, Diderot and d'Alembert's conversation, begins with the image of a swarm of bees described as a clump that appears as a being, an individual, an animal. It is evidently an illusion. It is an assemblage, but, if we blur the little legs the bees are holding on with, if we pass insensibly from contiguity to continuity, we can see a whole and an animal-one. We know it, not from d'Alembert, since he's dreaming, but from Doctor Bordeu who narrates d'Alembert's oneiric deliria to Melle de Lespinasse. Hence, he imagines the swarm of bees transformed into a veritable polyp and dreams, in the same vein, the human polyp. This puts you in the atmosphere of d'Alembert's dream where you see progressively the One become multiple in nature and the multiple as one, finally a perpetual reversibility from one to the other.

All this elides enormously at the end of d'Alembert's dream, since everything is found in the general flux: everything changes, everything passes, only the all remains, culminating in the One-all which stops at the boundaries of the world. Ultimately there is only one huge living animal which is nature itself: "And you speak of individuals? None exists. There is only a sole great individual, it is the all."

It happened that Lacan, precisely during the years when he was trying to give *jouissance* its stature, while he was presenting his lectures and pursuing his avocation of buying old books, looked through this materialist literature. He evoked Maupertuis.

This marks the distance we have come from the monism of matter, of a matter which includes life. Take, for example, Diderot, with his vitalist Spinozism in which everything, even stone, is supposed to be sensate. Thus he begins his conversation with d'Alembert, who says to him: "But you are not going to tell me that stone is sensate—But why not? It cries, we just don't hear it."

By degrees he demonstrates, appealing to nutrition, that mineral contributes to the growth of vegetable, and vegetable, absorbed by herbivore, finds itself in the living body. Thus we have an extraordinary continuity of sensibility, the same principle shared by the philosophies of nature which oblige us to distinguish two states of sensibility: one inert and one active, in which the inert (stone) may become active. This leads us also to the sensational 19th century lucubrations of Schelling on the ages of the world, in which consciousness is already encompassed in the notions of the inanimate, so that, in this world, the death of the individual is reduced to nothing more than an illusion.

HYLOZOISM

Says Diderot: "And life? Life, a series of actions and reactions. Living, I act and react in mass—mass of my body, the animalcules that form me. Dead, I act and react in molecules. Thus I don't die at all. No, without doubt. I don't die at all in this sense, neither myself nor whatever I'm made up of." It is a vision of life eternal if one doesn't stop at the imaginary form of the body, but rather allows the animalcules, the fibers, the molecules to continue their little journey.

In this way life and also *jouissance* are everywhere in nature. *Jouissance* is coextensive with omnipresent life. Citing Diderot: "There is nothing in nature which does not suffer or feel pleasure." There we have *jouissance* understood as all of nature and as each of its states. The word "hylozoism" dates from around 1760 in Diderot's *Encyclopedia*. This erudite word derives from hyle (matter) and *zoe* (life) and refers to the doctrine of living matter made God. And, as Lacan said, for the materialists of the 18th century, their God was matter.

Amazingly enough, the idea of the great living and immortal All was also the doctrine of the stoics, the very ones who invented the difference between the signifier and the signified. How could they, on the one hand, use language to articulate and disarticulate, while on the other hand adhere simultaneously to this doctrine of the great animate world and of life everywhere? Here we have proof that they apprehended the unity of the signifier One at the level of language, because in nature, they only apprehended the unity of the All. And this supports Lacan's thesis that one apprehends the One from the signifier and not from nature. The closer you get, the more you see what One is made of. We have every reason to use hylozoism as a point of reference in the question we are advancing, since it is clearly the implicit basis of Sade's theory elaborated by Lacan in the section of *The Ethics of Psychoanalysis*[4] on transgression and *jouissance* in transgression. Sade refers to the system of Pope Pius VI, the criminal Pope whose postulate is that nature itself desires destruction, death. Sade distinguished in this regard two deaths: that of the individual, who is already *jouissance*, having finished with the other, and that of the matter itself, of the cadaver which results from the death of the individual. You find Sade's text on pages 210-211 of his Seminar VII. The radical criminal wants not only to be the other at the level of life, of the individual body, but also in the matter that subsists after the first crime. Diderot's hylozoism is the basis of the theory of two deaths.

The idea of two deaths is like the two sides of Diderot's double life: "Living, I act and react in mass. Dead, I act and react in molecules." Diderot's system is the exact reverse of Sade's. Sade gives us the first and second death; Diderot the first and second life.

2. THE EMERGENCE OF THE BODY IN PIECES
DESCARTES AND SUBSTANCE-*JOUISSANCE*

Lacan refers to Descartes to introduce life-*jouissance* or what he calls substance-*jouissance*. This is the opposite of hylozoism, because there is no question of living matter. He is not going to look for it in Diderot's *jouissance*, which is everywhere, universal, in every point in nature. We do not lack different levels of material in Diderot's work; we have continuous praise of the infinite possibilities of *jouissance*, from the most minuscule and insensible to the most vast. Descartes, however, reduces matter to thought, and this reduction excludes by principle the *jouissance* of body, since body emerges from thought.

And so Lacan can say, in his text "De la psychanalyse dans ses rapports avec la realité"[5] that the body, reduced to thought, was profoundly misunderstood by Descartes. The constitutive misunderstanding of the reduction of matter and body to thought is in separating the body from its *jouissance*. But one must state at that the misunderstanding is also found in the operations to which we currently submit the body more and more frequently.

I read a kind of prophesy in what Lacan wrote in 1967 on this subject: "with the shocks of the imminent excesses of our surgery, we are disposed to make the body into its own pieces." It is not only that the being of life is not the One of the individual, but also that the being of life, when the body is a speaking being, is this body in pieces. This is not the profusion of Diderot: "We are all polyparies, we are all colonies of animalcules badly individuated." It is the One put in question by the body in pieces.

AN ESSAY OF SWIFTIAN INSPIRATION

The body in pieces—we know it at the level of *fantasme*. It is the expression Lacan coined in order to put in parentheses the imaginary phenomena on which Melanie Klein insisted. We are talking about the body in pieces as realized through surgical operation. Biology, having celebrated the unity of the living over a long period of time, now distinguishes itself every day with the dismemberment (*morcellement*) of this unity.

Just today I came upon an extraordinary essay in this week's *Time* magazine. You know that we can transplant the most important organs, since the epochal heart transplant of Dr. Barnard. The problem today is that we do not have enough of these organs to transplant. 62,000 Americans are waiting for organs in order to survive! Who will give them these organs?

The author of this *Time* article has an idea—we must buy them. Of course there must be someone to sell them. So, a sensational proposition: authorize families to sell the organs of their deceased.

There is an objection. Only the poorest people will be tempted to sell the kidneys and the hearts of their dear departed for

$300—the value the author proposes. The response to that is: all suffering in the world affects the poor more than the rich. The poor live less well, they dress less well, they have the most dangerous jobs, and they have the smallest cars. Thus, if one insists, we can pay them $3,000 rather than $300. The audacious author admits a limit: he doesn't propose buying the organs of the living, because that would be an affront to human dignity.

This little text which happened to fall into my hands by accident is of Swiftian inspiration. You know Swift's *A Modest Proposal*: "how to ease parents and the nation of their charges and use these children for the public good?" Swift's text proposes that one year old children contribute to the public good, to the diet and in part to the attire of several thousand people. He proposes that they be eaten. Swift's work is a satire on the cynicism of the wealthy of his time; it is strikingly similar to the American essay which seriously approaches such action.

For the public good and the individual good

Thus we announce the emergence of the body in pieces. We can say *au revoir* to what has been the celebration of the unity of the body, since what is in progress is the contrary, its cutting up, evidently for the greater good. Every day we have news of the body in pieces. A more amiable form of cutting up permitted by genetic genius. We speak of genetic genius because we cannot stop at the image of the beautiful form of the body, since we know how to operate on the real of the body. Tissues can be engineered. Skin has been made and sold since May of 1998. Last year fabricated skin was approved for sale. Cartilage and bone can be produced with the help of semi-synthetic material. Ligaments and tendons are at the ready, but the great object of study now is the creation of complete internal organs, neo-organs.

These phenomena impart a special seriousness to what we can articulate about our relationship to body, which is not transhistoric, and our work will be more and more conditioned by this emergence of the body in pieces. It is no longer a matter of the nasty Marquis de

Sade who is going to cut up poor Justine. It is evidently for the public good and the individual good, that is to say it is irresistible.

The assemblage of some elements of Lacanian biology should be useful here. Let us take a look at the algorithms of life.

THE BODY-MACHINE

The Cartesian element here is what is anti-Aristotelian. The former proceeds from a perspective that dissects the unity of the living, while the Aristotelian view emphasizes the unity of living, the soul as a form of the body. In his Seminar *Encore* Lacan contrasts these two perspectives by referring repeatedly to Aristotle's *On the Soul* and at the same time measuring developments in biology which influence the philosophical form of our imaginary of the body, already out of date because of the effects of the algorithms of life.

This Aristotelian perspective is hopelessly dated. Lacan considered, regardless, that a whole branch of contemporary philosophy was devoted to reinflating, to redesigning this Aristotelian perspective for current consumption. Gestalts, the psychology of form, Goldsteinism, and even being-in-the-world, or the phenomenology of perception, consistently attempted to return to the harmony of the soul and its body. Descartes in other words was a brute to have made two separate substances and they were going to occupy themselves sewing it up to recover the unity of life.

Lacan, neither progressive, so he says, nor nostalgic, knows that one will go always too far in the Cartesian sense, that is to say to operate on the body, to dismantle it like a machine.

Following his Seminar II, he underlines the decisive character of reference to the machine as the foundation of biology. This dismantling, this cutting up proceeds essentially from distancing what is the marvellous harmony of the living organism in its milieu in order to operate and dislocate, dismember and disarticulate.

Surprisingly François Jacob writes: "Molecular biology corresponds to a new mechanical age." Conceptually, we are not in this mechanist scheme because we have new information or because we are operating on the molecular level. There are sensational changes in biology, but at the same time some phenomena have persisted for a long time and this scheme is one of them. Something proceeding from Descartes' animal-machine is still there.

We will see how Freud oriented his biology in essential background research. The facts of dismemberment question the identity of the body in a much more probing way than the hylozoist lucubrations or the Aristotelian soul which is only, as Lacan says on page 110 of *Encore*, the supposed identity of the body.

THE SPEAKING BODY EMERGES FROM HAVING

We have learned something fundamental about the status of the body, of this body which gives the imaginary model of One. We identify the body and the being of life in some spontaneous, imaginary way. Lacan describes this in passing while talking about the rat in the labyrinth in the last chapter of the Seminar *Encore*. We can identify there the body and the being (*être*). This identification is in Aristotle's initial analysis of being. Today, on the contrary, we try to confuse the poor little rat, immersing it in the knowledge of the experimenter, a knowledge which has nothing to do with its life.

If we can identify being and body for the animal, we cannot do the same for the human species. As far as the speaking body is concerned, it does not emerge from being but from having.

Lacan puts a surprising touch on the formula "man has a body," which is incarnated in English law under the formula of habeas corpus. He expounds on "man has a body" in one of his last texts, "Joyce-the-symptom,"[6] but you find it already in Seminar II, page 73. He notes moreover that one has always had a body, but it is clearer today, because we have gone very far from the identification of man with his knowledge.

Here we can make sense of the background of Cartesian dualism. The dualism here is of knowledge and of body. The question of being for "man" is posed on the side of knowledge, while the body is on the side of having. This identification of man with his knowledge is what made Lacan culminate with the concept of the algorithm of the subject. His position is on the order of being, even if it is formulated as lack-in-being.

One can say again more simply that the subject, from the moment in which it is subject of the signifier, cannot identify itself as its body, and it is precisely from there that its affection for the image of its body proceeds. The enormous narcissistic bombast, characteristic of the species, proceeds from this lack of subjective identification with the body. The lack of corporeal identification is especially in evidence in hysteria. Lacan constantly critiques, implicitly or explicitly, the phenomenology of Merleau-Ponty who tries to restore the co-naturalness of man to his world, who centers on the corporeal presence, who studies presence in the world in, by, and through a body. This presence is also evident in Heidegger's philosophy of the *Dasein*, where it is displaced in accordance with what it has circumvented. The presupposition, as Lacan says, for Merleau-Ponty, is that there is somewhere a place of unity, which is the identification of the being and body, and which has as result the effacement of the subject. If one sees things in this perspective, behaviorism is susceptible to the same critique. Even if the phenomenalists and the gestalt psychologists make sport of Watson, the idea of describing behavior in terms of stimulus-response, leaving aside all introspection, rests finally on an equivalence of being and body. Psychoanalysis makes its space in the lack of this identification between being and body, in maintaining that the subject has a relationship of having with the body.

3. FREUD'S BIOLOGY

Freud put a lot of hope in biology. I quote: "Biology is truly a land of unlimited possibilities. We may expect it to give us the most surprising information and we cannot guess what answers it will return in a few dozen years to the questions we have put to it."[7]

THE OTHER SIDE OF LIFE OPEN TO THE SPEAKING BODY

Lacan, in the context in which he examined speech, posited that Freudian biology was not biology. Death, which is a matter of the death drive, is not biological death; it is not the simple return of the living body to an inanimate state. Death is the other side of life. A biology which includes the death drive is a biology of the other side of life, an other side which is open to the speaking being through language. This other side of life is materialized through the sepulcher, since the human species is the only one in which the dead body keeps its value. Sade himself is the example of this other side of life which is open to the speaking body. He dreamed of the death of molecules. He dreamed of a criminal who could, beyond the individual, kill molecules. Practically, as we know, he demanded in his will that his proper name be effaced on his tombstone.

What is specifically of man must last, not in the form of molecules, but in the form of signifiers. Sade wanted to attain this signifying margin on the other side of life and disappear. Sade's demand, and even his injunction, his death drive, has a bearing on the signifier and has nothing to do with biology.

WEISMANN'S CONCEPTUAL SCHEME

But Freudian biology is all the same a biology. At least it supported its speculation with biology, and it did not make a bad choice with Weismann and his theory of germ plasm. The great reference is chapter VI of *Beyond the Pleasure Principle*.

We must recognize the relationship between Weismann's germ and the present-day genome. Doubtless the germ and the genome are inscribed in different discourses. Weismann's is pure speculation and Freud is interested in the attempts to show Weismann's theory as experimentation. Watson and Crick are truly inscribed in a science, molecular genetics. The science leads to practice and emerges with genetic genius. The same scheme between Weismann's germ and Watson and Crick's genome is of no hindrance to us. The same conceptual scheme is at work between the research that Freud chose in biology, our present biology, and that of the future.

I found this fact pleasantly confirmed in the beginning of a reading of a slightly iconoclastic epistemology, André Pichot's

*L'histoire de la notion de gène*. Weismann had no idea that *mutatis mutandis* the substance which transported heredity, the chromosomes, would be part of the same conceptual scheme that remains in the work of biology decades later. After some purely physical considerations on statistical laws, Erwin Schrödinger, in a small popular book of 1944, *What is life?*, anticipated exactly the concept of molecular genetics. Pichot says that Schrödinger gives the theoretical basis ten years before the elaboration of the structure of DNA. Departing from Weismann, enriched by chromosomal theory, Schrödinger deduces what will take form in 1953 in the double helix of Watson and Crick, putting us in the perspectives of the next century in which the relationship of the body and its dismemberment will be expanded.

Freud is brought to the central axis of biology as if by divination. Even the neo-Darwinists of today refer to Weismann. The talented popularizer, Richard Dawkins, the author of *The Selfish Gene*, writes at length: "The central idea that I have used has been outlined by Weismann." What Freud deduced is truly the point of departure of the central route of biology today. In chapter VI of *Beyond the Pleasure Principle* Freud explains the theory of the two categories of drives: the death drive seeking to restore the inanimate state and the life drive, or sex drive, tending toward sexual conjunction and to "the coalescence of two germ-cells which are differentiated, tending to assure reproduction, to prolong the cell's life and to lend it the appearance of immortality." He finds an analogy of Weismann's to support his elaboration of the life drive and death drive. "The greatest interest attaches from our point of view to the treatment given to the subject of the duration of life and the death of organisms in the writings of Weismann. He was he who introduced the division of living substance into mortal and immortal parts. The mortal part is the body in the narrower sense— the soma—which alone is subject to natural death. The germ-cells, on the other hand, are potentially immortal, in so far as they are able, under certain favorable conditions, to develop into a new individual, or, in other words, to surround themselves with a new soma."[8]

What is the notion in question? There are two kinds of differentiated cells, those specializing in reproduction, the others developing into individual bodies. On the one hand, the germ cells of reproduction persist and are transmitted in some way as an autonomous lineage. Jacob himself says: "The reproduction of unicellular beings is by simple fission, and each is capable of giving birth to a body, of encompassing an individual body, a soma, which is in some way an end in itself." A lineage is perpetuated while the individual body is grafted in some way on this lineage:

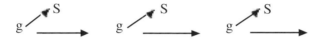

This is intuition along with Weismann's conceptual scheme, with reproduction entirely dependent on nature and the properties of the germ. And everything that happens to the individual body in the point of view of heredity is completely indifferent to lineage and disappears with it, while "natural selection operates on the hidden dispositions of the germ cell." Heredity appears here separated from any incident, and, adds François Jacob, "from all desire."

The royal road of biology proceeds from this simple scheme. It is surrounded by Weismann's philosophy, a philosophy of biophore (he thinks there are particles carrying life in germ-cells) but these are just flourishes which add nothing of force to the scheme. In effect, in a whole other context, what one finds as the structure of DNA comes from Weismann's germ.

THE NARCISSISTIC GERM-CELL

What interests Freud here is the analogy which has him impose the life drive on the germ and the death drive on the soma. He situates his theory of the drives here. Of course he notes that psychoanalysis is not interested in the life substance but in the forces that operate in the life substance, and these are the drives. He presents the theory of the drives as the dynamic that completes Weismann's morphology. He is interested in detail in the trials of experimental demonstrations of this thesis. What disturbs him is very striking. What disturbs him is that Weismann shows unicellular organisms in which the soma and the germ are not different, are potentially immortal. It is a well supported concept today: the immortality of the initial bacteria, of the mother of all bacteria. What disturbs Freud is that the somatic death only intervenes in the pluricellular, that is to say that death is a late acquisition. He says: "There can be no question of there having been death drives from the very beginning of life on this earth."[9]

We must follow in this chapter Freud's really hair pulling reasoning to try to show that the protozoans could very well sustain the death drives from the beginning without being perceived as doing so. It is a truly refined demonstration, but it shows that what counts for him is the doctrine of life itself. The question of *jouissance* which inhabits this matter of the death drive has to be linked for him to life as such. Thus the importance of remembering, with Lacan, we are interested in *jouissance* as linked to life but under the form of the body.

Freud's whole effort wants to show that these drives are already present independent of the constitution, not only of a body, but even of a multicelled organism. He manages finally, maneuvering, to validate his analogy with Weismann. He invents the egoist gene. He invents neo-Darwinism. The idea of the potentially immortal gene which uses individual bodies to self-perpetuate—the chicken appears as the means the egg has found to produce another egg, according to the philosopher Butler quoted by Jacob—is such a Freudian framework that he even speaks of the narcissism of the germ: the germ cells act in an absolutely narcissistic way in the sense of psychoanalysis. The notion of the narcissistic germ is the prefiguration of contemporary neo-Darwinism found in Dawkins' bestselling *The Selfish Gene*.

What is the idea of the selfish gene? Dawkins has the gene speak. The gene tries to survive and to reproduce, so it programs bodies to that end. So far, so good. But, it becomes startling when the genetic population is dispersed throughout numerous individuals, creating a genetic solidarity. He then studies the behavior of the body while deducing from it the egoism of the gene. If parents protect their children, it is in order to protect the genes. And on from there to love and social life. The gene that moves everything to self-perpetuate and achieve its goals is everywhere. In the same vein, you have, after the 70s sociobiology.

In a short circuit, in his introduction to what would become the Department of Psychoanalysis, Lacan curiously qualifies the imaginary and the real as "space of life" (*lieu de la vie*): "My imaginary and my real, through which are distinguished two spaces of life that science to this date strictly separates." How can one say that the imaginary and the real are spaces of life? The concept rests on the distinction germ/soma. The imaginary is tied to the individual body, while the germ, and especially the genome, is the space of life, the real of life.

Perhaps even more startling as a short circuit is Lacan's analogy found on page 90 of *Encore*: "The function I give the letter is what makes it analogous to a germ." Lacan reworks the following scheme, making the letter analogous to the germ. It is Weismann's germ Lacan brings to molecular physiology. It has surpassed this term "germ" since he speaks of the germ separate from the bodies for which it is the vehicle for life and death together.

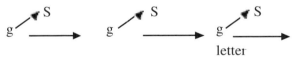
letter

This analogy of the letter and the germ is evidently made to give us the notion of a reproduction of the letter, but which supposes the exteriority of knowledge (*savoir*) in relationship to being, in relationship to body. It is a transmission of the letter, but in a position of exteriority. Thus Lacan says: "Knowledge (*savoir*) is in the Other. It is a knowledge which is supported by the signifier and which owes nothing to the knowing (*connaissance*) of life (*vivant*)."

## II. LIFE AS CONDITION OF *JOUISSANCE*
translated by JORGE JAUREGUI

My sole interest for life is its connection to *jouissance* in as much as it could be that life is what deserves to be qualified as real. I believe Lacan's propositions do not object the formulation that life is the condition of *jouissance*. If life is condition of *jouissance*, it is a necessary condition, not a sufficient one. I've been careful to distinguish life as such, to not say as force, and the body. Life overflows the body. What obliges you to attest there isn't *jouissance* unless life appears under the form of a living body.

### 1. BODY CONDITION AND SIGNIFIER CONDITION

Let's examine the proposition. What that the living body says to us? It says that the case is not only the imaginary body, under the form of its form. The case is not the body image, the one we know, to which we refer to since it is operative in the mirror stage— the specular body that doubles the organism. It is neither the symbolic body, the one whose persistent recurrence prompts the heraldry metaphor under Lacan's pen. Coat of arms are codes. Body parts can certainly be represented, beside with other natural elements, yet they account for signifiers. They are imaginary signifiers whose matter is taken from the image. When we say "the living body," we leave aside both the symbolized body and the body image. The body affected by *jouissance* is neither imaginary nor symbolic, but a living one. Nothing prevents locating *jouissance* as an affect of the body, and the question is to give this adjective that cannot be elided, its sense, alive, for us so less precise than the imaginary or the symbolic adjective. These echo Lacan's teaching and may after all be founded under epistemology and even under the works of history of science that he used to support his distinction between the imaginary and the symbolic, whereas the living enters our discourse without being the least endowed with that incomparable precision.

The question is to give this adjective of the living its sense and also of detecting in which way, through which incidence, the affect of *jouissance* starts in the body. We have then, if we admit this perspective, the condition of the body.

I can at once mention a second condition that adds to the condition of body so that something like the sufficient condition be attained. It is the signifier condition, if we settle for Lacan's formula that the signifier is cause of *jouissance*. Thus the perspective—life as condition of *jouissance*, the condition of body, the condition of signifier—I will explore in this Lacanian biology.

At the end of it there is a clinic that revolves on a definition I believe has been neglected from the symptom, thus fundamental, that must be addressed. It is the one of the symptom as event of the body, which appears at least once in Lacan. If it has been neglected, it's for sure that it looks partial. The symptom as event of the body seems to neglect evidence, as in the case of the obsessional symptom excelling as symptom of the mind, even though the obsessional symptom of the mind is always accompanied by corporal symptoms. And then, the definition of the symptom as event of the body stands for an impasse on every other symptom that, in the different clinical structures, affect par excellence the mind, the uttered, language. It is thus a logical definition of the symptom, of which we are not prone to escape much as we apprehend the symptom as *jouissance*, even when we apprehend it in the Freudian terms of *Inhibition, Symptom and Anxiety*, as drive satisfaction. If the symptom is drive satisfaction, if it is *jouissance* as conditioned by life under the form of the body, that implies that the living body prevails in every symptom.

This is the horizon of what I call Lacanian biology: the recapture of the symptomatology from the body events. However, this will demand some redefinitions, certain precisions that seemingly prevent the definition to be considered as operative.

## 2. From Drives' Dualism to Drive's Monism
### The split of death

To well measure what I have spoken apropos life and its materialistic myths, I'll say something about death. In relation to death, it is the right moment to settle up Lacan's saying that Freudian biology has nothing to do with biology. Let's clean up Lacan's distinction between Freudian biology and biology in strict sense. It led Lacan to identify two deaths from the system of Pope Pius VI which appears in Sade's Juliette. The first death, in this cogitation, is the one to strike life off the individual body and transform it into a corpse. The second is the one that will strike the molecules of the body reduced to corpse. You should reread this split of death. The Lacanian split is not the Sadean split. It finds support on the Sadean split, but is not subdued by it. The two deaths existence supposes the existence of two lives or of two forms of life: the first one takes place under the form of the body and the second one under a form infra, infra-corporal, a molecular life. The Sadean speculation relies on this materialistic vitalism, encouraging what we may call "the crime", which would be the desire to strike not only to the first life but also to the molecular life.

If we distance ourselves from the criminal passion animating the above mentioned speculation, the scheme of the split is outlined this way: a death beyond death, a life beyond life. Nevertheless, both in Diderot and in Sade, the double life and the double death belong to the biological register. A dreamed biology. The dichotomy thus introduced affects the actual difference (that exists) between life and the death. The split Lacan canvasses in his Ethics of Psychoanalysis is based on the fact that life as such overflows the life of the individual body and that the body is but a transitory form, a perishable form of life. Sade's *Wunsch*, which ultimately Lacan calls death drive, aims at life as such beyond the body. When we speak of Sade, who is the carrier of such a name? It is the subject that assumes, that takes for itself the death drive, subjetctifying it as a crime, and extending it up to the elements of the rotten body of which it desires its disappearance, its annihilation. Do we find something similar in Freud? If Lacan looked in Sade for the biological split, he did so because there is no track of this split in Freud. Freud does not distinguish between life and the body.

REPETITION, A FACTOR OF MALADJUSTMENT

Let's look into chapter V of *Beyond the Pleasure Principle* where Freud develops what he will term in 1925 an extreme line of thought, one susceptible of amendment and rectification.

What is this extreme line? It consists, firstly, in attributing the clinical compulsion to repetition to the living body, to the living organism as such, or even to the living substance; secondly, envisaging this repetition as a tendency towards the re-establishment of a previous state; thirdly, in identifying this state anterior to death as (with) no-life, that is biological death in as much as the non-living was there before the living. The demonstration attempted by Freud in chapters V and VI isolates a movement towards death that would affect the living as such. For him the individual body obeys (follows) the same logic (rationale) that governs life as such. Besides, it is what leads him to look for the manifestations of these drives since the origin of life. What comes up in Freud as the initial state, the natural state, is the inanimate state, as far as it is a state without tension, and life appears as an exterior disturbance arising in the inanimate. Freud says it explicitly in this extreme speculation: "The properties of life were roused in the inanimate matter by the action of a force." He asserts himself that this force is truly unthinkable for us. He is still arguing with the vitalism that haunts the biology of his time. Lacan, coherent with his point of departure, at once denies biological relevancy to death, conceived as the return of the animate to the inanimate. He develops it in Seminar II.

What forces Freud to think about death as fate of the living seized by a repetition which entails a bias towards death? What forces him to introduce this conception? What forces Freud to think of that, says Lacan, it is not the death of living beings but human life. By this expression he deems human exchange, intersubjectivity, the fact of language. On the one side Lacan admits repetition as a clinical phenomenon, yet, on the other, he bestows a complete different meaning to the connection between repetition and death.

Where Freud, in his extreme speculation, perceives repetition as an originally vital phenomenon, Lacan doesn't. The Lacanian repetition is not coming from the behavior of the living organism. It is not a vital phenomenon but an anti-vital one, much as according to Freudian speculation in the human species repetition opposes adaptation. Repetition and adaptation are two important registers at times pursued with difficulty, yet persistently, along this paper of Lacan.

All animal psychology celebrates the adaptation of the animal organism to its milieu. Von Uexküll enliven reference is permanent with Lacan: he shows for instance the way the fly owns a world to itself by apprehending from the environment significant spaces to which it appears gloriously adapted. Adaptation culminates there in harmony. Therefore adaptation, fitting, or, as Lacan argues in "L'étourdit," trait by trait rapport between the *Umwelt* and the *Innenwelt*, between the exterior world and the animal's interior world. Thus, a perfect inside/out between the organism and its milieu.

It is in relation to this important experimental concept, arising from observation, that repetition, by contrast, takes on its dimension. It's in relation to this wonderful, harmonic adaptation, that Freudian repetition re-read by Lacan takes on relief, to the extent that you don't have to be a witch doctor to show that repetition is, for the human kind, a factor of failure to adapt; that repetition such as it originates in the clinic, appears fundamentally as determining a maladjusted behavior in relation to life requirements, to the well-being of the body.

What Freud calls need of repetition, far from being a need like any other one appears on the contrary as an disharmonic constraint concerning the living being as such. In this respect Lacan admits the fact of repetition. He demonstrates that with regard to adaptation, repetition belongs to a register which is not at all biological, yet can only be thought in the register of language. This is already outlining, in *Beyond the Pleasure Principle*, the place of the superego as principle of anti-vital repetition.

THE SUPEREGO'S DRIVE

This is what leads Freud to introduce his concept of the superego—till then related to what suited self-preservation in the living being—in the exact lieu of the ego. Thus he equates the drives of the ego to the drives of the living being sufficing its subsistence. In chapter V of *Beyond the Pleasure Principle* you see Freud's embarrassment with the term of the ego drives; throughout his difficult argumentation the drives of the ego become the drive of death. He starts putting the drives of the ego in brackets. He states, nevertheless, about 1925, in *Inhibitions, Symptoms and Anxiety*, that it is just a provisory appellation simply rooted in the first Freudian terminology. The drive of death, as it looms in Freud's text, is the drive of the superego. Self-preservation, in itself a prerogative of the ego and a reissue of the Aristotelian soul, is dissolved. What emerges instead is a drive that restores the living to death—the opposite of self-preservation. Lacan reads it like detours of the signifying system, which is the Freudian name for the superego. There is in Freud, supported and valued as such, a dualism of drives. There is death drive, which I translate as drive of the superego, and there is the sexual drives, life drives adverse to the drives that lead to death—hence they are not drives of self-preservation, but of reproduction. Freud bases this dualism on Weismann's biology, on the difference between soma and the germ-cell.

A REUNIFIED DRIVE

Here we can question the place of libido between the death drive and the sexual drives. This place seems particularly complex since, on one side, libido is present in so called self-preservation drives that refer to the ego as reservoir of libido, yet on the other it is equally present in the sexual drives that preserve life. To this effect Freud remarks that the opposition between drives of the ego and sexual drives proves to be inadequate, and he intends to rebuff the inconvenience which consists in locating the libido inside the dualism and replacing this opposition by that of life drives and the death drive.

You must notice the striking transformation that Lacan performs on this theory of drives allegedly grounded on biology. When we say drive we are not taking into account, in spite of Freud's repeated warnings, the dualism of the drives: Lacan's perspective outclasses the dualism of the drives. Lacan takes great pains to extract the drive as such from what Freud accepted under the form of this dualism. Besides he surrounds it with all the precautions so as to render infeasible its avoidance so pretext that by doing so you would fall down into Jungism, pansexuality, etc.

Often I spoke about the drives in Lacan without underlining the evident and major fact that he annuls the Freudian dualism of the drives. He says it his way, discreetly, in *The Four Fundamental Concepts*: "The distinction between the life drive and the death drive is true in as much as it manifests two aspects of the drive. But all the sexual drives bring out death as signifier."[10] He is even clearer in the contemporary *écrit* to the above mentioned Seminar, "Position de l'inconscient" where he argues that "every drive is virtually drive of death."[11] This means but the annulment of the Freudian dualism. He represents it to us under the form of his myth of the lamella, which is a mythical representation of the libido. He draws his inspiration from the reference Freud takes from Plato's *Banquet* so to fashion his myth from that of Aristophanes. He represents for us the libido as an organ, as an object, but an object endowed with a deadly sense. He defines the libido under the form of the myth, as a being carrier of death.

Lacan's complex exertion touches on both death and libido. It consists in showing that death is by no means the prerogative of the death drive, that it is present in the sexual drives and, symmetrically, the libido is present in the death drive. This double demonstration, scattered along Lacan's teaching, finally results in the annulment of the dualism of the drives as well as allowing us today to say "the drive." Freud himself indicates that the libido is found in the death drive when he defines, in chapter V, repetition as repetition of a primary satisfaction, a somehow washed out and inadequate repetition. Straightaway he posits failure as the foundation of repetition. The satisfaction attained by repetition is not equivalent to the mandatory satisfaction. There is always a deficit. Here Freud perceives the origin of what shoves ahead the human being, of what precludes satisfaction in any established situation, forcing him to move ahead in his path towards death, before the aim of a complete satisfaction could be attained.

The essential Freudian dichotomy is re-absorbed somehow by Lacan who evinces that death and the libido have close links. This is the real sense of his myth of the lamella: the libido is a deadly being. This formula distorts, gets over the boundaries Freud established for the dualism he drags with him ever since the difference between drives of the ego and sexual drives, and life drives and death drive. This monism of the drive is certainly a moment of consequence in Lacan's teaching. His point of departure is eminently binary: language and libido, symbolic and imaginary. The very movement of his teaching rolls towards the production of monist categories. Somehow we witness entire sections of his teachings collapse when these monist categories arise, the first of which is that of a reunified drive.

1. Jacob, François, *The Logic of Life*, NJ: Princenton Univ. Press, 1993.
2. Lacan, Jacques, *The Seminar, Book II: The Ego in Freud's Theory and in the Technique of Psychoanalysis, 1954-1955*, NY: Norton, 1988.
3. Lacan, J., *The Seminar, Book XX: On Feminine Sexuality, The Limits of Love and Knowledge: Encore, 1972-1973*, NY: Norton, 1998.
4. Lacan, J., *The Seminar, Book VII: The Ethics of Psychoanalysis, 1959-1960*, NY: Norton, 1992.
5. Lacan., J., "De la psychanalyse dans ses rapports avec la realité," in *Scilicet*, Paris, 1969.
6. Lacan, J., "Joyce, le symptôme," in *L'Ane*, Paris, 1982.
7. Freud, Sigmund, *Beyond the Pleasure Principle*, S.E. XVIII, London: The Hogarth Press, 1986.
8. ibid
9. ibid
10. Lacan, J., *The Seminar, Book XI: The Four Fundamental Concepts of Psychoanalysis, 1964*, NY: Norton, 1978.
11. Lacan, J., "Position de l'inconscient," in *Écrits*, Paris: Seuil, 1966.

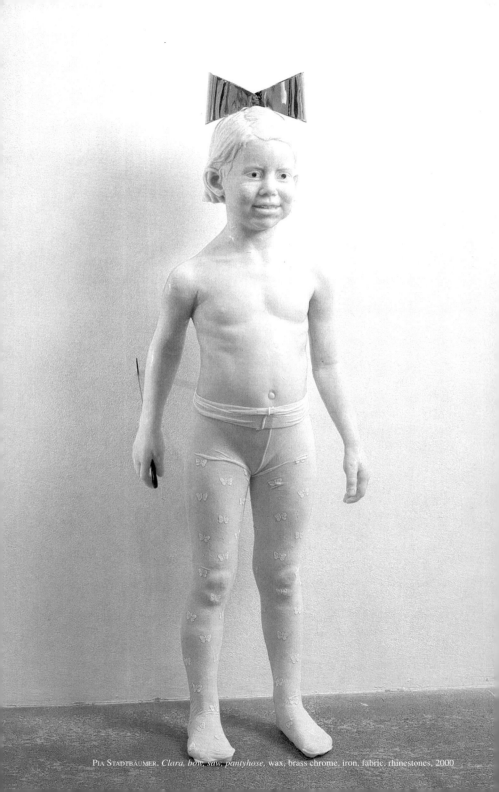

Pia Stadtbäumer, *Clara, bow, saw, pantyhose,* wax, brass chrome, iron, fabric, rhinestones, 2000

# Gender and Sexuation

RICHARD KLEIN

Gender is briefly discussed and contrasted with the equivalent in the teaching of Lacan, namely, sexuation, which, of course, is not an equivalence that exists since gender implies a sexual relation between the man and the woman, and sexuation is based on the impossibility of establishing the sexual relation between the two sexes. It goes further in sexuation: the *heteros* is missing.

There are gender effects in the dialectic of being and having the phallus which is a function that makes up for the absent sexual relation.[1] Having the phallus is the centrepiece in Freud's doctrine of masculinity. Being the phallus is Lacan's invention in 1958 based on Riviere's masquerade.[2] Masculinity is the result of one kind of relation to the phallus, and femininity of another kind to it. One signifier, two sexes, or, as one says now, two genders! This dialectic begins with symbolic support but is eventually devalued to the imaginary. What does that mean? It means that masculinity and femininity can be described. Do descriptions lead to an essence? According to Riviere the masquerade is definitely not the essence of femininity.

The fundamental trauma is no longer castration which the phallus includes. Traumatic is the sexual non-rapport in that the sexual relation is a hole in the real. It is *troumatique*.[3] Nothing like a hole to indicate that something that does not exist can still operate. The sexual relation does not exist, and it is the source of symptoms. If gender can be counted amongst these symptoms, then the non-rapport may also be a source of gender which is, in any case, a prosthetic device as all identifications are. That's no reason not to use them to make up for what does not exist.

If this is the same real that one makes oneself the dupe of, then it becomes part of the ethics of psychoanalysis. A dupe can err just as much as a non-dupe. One must not be a dupe of just anything. In the ethics of psychoanalysis one has to make oneself a dupe of a disturbing knowledge since from the unconscious one strays beyond the fantasy into the real[4] to which one can only have a solitary relation, based, as it is, on our exile from the Other sex.

Jacques-Alain Miller uses a term he calls connection-operator in his discussion of the sixth paradigm of *jouissance*.[5] It may prove interesting to extend its use in the present discussion of the sexual non-rapport. "The impossibility of writing the sexual relation at the level of the real"—this phrase is, nevertheless, a signifier from which a signified can be extracted, namely, the disconnection between the man and the woman. It's one of the main points elaborated in Seminar XX.[6]

It seems to me to be less ambiguous to refer to a disconnection between the man and the woman, as blunt as Lacan is: "...the impossibility of inscribing the sexual relation between two bodies of different sexes."[7] Translating "rapport" as symmetry would certainly lead to ambiguity. That would provide us with sexual non-symmetry or dissymmetry in the sexual relation. However, at least two parties are involved in a dissymmetry with effects in the symbolic and imaginary. In other words, a dissymmetry is not a disconnection. A disconnection is real. Nevertheless, in the symbolic there are many complex relations between the man and the woman, some of them dissymmetric, such as the relation in the dialectic of being and having the phallus. These relations may be interrupted before ever arriving at a specific, real disconnection. Narcissistic reasons abound in the interruption of such relations. But, perhaps narcissistic connections are being caused by a disconnection.

Given a disconnection between the man and the woman, one might wish to inquire about a previous connection. In the myth of the Name-of-the-Father such a connection is made. The connection is mythical. The subject craves for it which must account for the success of religious discourse. The disconnection is a fault in the structure concealed by the myth which structures truth like fiction. Fiction becomes our truth in a discourse. The effects of a fault in the structure are outside the discourse and has to be concealed by something else, by the reference.

The sexual relation, he says on Seminar XX,[8] is not working out and is working out anyway. There is a disconnection and a connection anyway. The left-hand side of the table of sexuation is the connection-side, the fiction side. The right-hand side the disconnection side with the only possible partner for both sexes, the reference. For we can also talk about the table of sexuation as sense and reference. That is, evidently, what he means by a sexual relation that is not working out but is working out anyway. He has got it balanced in the table of sexuation between disconnection and connection. The Borromean knot which comes next in his teaching allows this balance to continue in the knot itself.

Before it is enciphered in the Borromean knot, Lacan logicises the disconnection modally as that which does not cease not being written, which is impossible. The connection is logicised as that which ceases not being written, which is contingent. Contingency appears in his teaching at least as early as 1958 in relation to the subject's existence as a woman or as a man. In our modern psychology they are gender terms which are, Lacan says, contingent with respect to existence, except he uses the term *sexe*.[9]

When it is working out, the operator is the big Other. A contingent connection occurs between the man and the woman in the field of the Other under the aegis of the paternal metaphor:

$$NF(Other/phallus)$$

The connection-operators are the Other and the phallus. In the paternal metaphor one is led to believe that the disconnection ceases not to be written. However, the disconnection does not cease not to be written. The disconnection side unceasingly separates from the connection side, and the connection side unceasingly reabsorbs the disconnection side. The phallic function ceases not to be written and submits the sexual relation to the regime of the encounter.[10] The impossible sexual relation is replaced with another term, the sexual encounter, which is contingent. But, it seems, we don't follow this policy uniformly.

The matheme $S(\cancel{A})$ is a disconnection-operator. It is the Other as *l'Une-en-moins*, the One-missing as it has now been translated.[11] Maybe that way of putting it—as the One-missing—has the ring of a disconnection. One can also index on it the interpretation "not everything can be said," or the Other is not-wholly in the discourse. When the Other is not-wholly in the discourse, we write $S(\cancel{A})$.

It's the Other that does not exist and is the sign of a disconnection. The woman, says Lacan in Seminar XX,[12] is not-whole in that something in her escapes discourse. At the point a woman is not-wholly in the discourse the disconnection-operator is dominant, and she is in a relation to $S(\cancel{A})$.

The man seeks out the woman in so far as she can be situated in discourse.[13] He does not seek her out as not-all. In discourse the woman is a signifier *quoad matrem*.[14] That makes sense for him. She enters the sexual relation as mother, having sought out a man as signifier. As a signifier the man enters the sexual relation *quoad castrationem*, and is in a relation to phallic *jouissance.*[15] In the table of sexuation the man is incarnated in the signifier Φ. It is a signifier of castrated *jouissance*. The man and the woman seek each other out as connection-operators. Those terms which designate gender, masculinity and femininity, but, evidently, not core gender identity, are derived from Oedipal connection-operators, namely, from the signifiers mother and father. A connection is made in what Lacan calls a sexual encounter. In an encounter gender ceases not to be written. Gender is the sexed body which includes the secondary sex characteristics which are those of the mother.[16] In the sexual encounter gender involves a prohibited body which is separated from *jouissance*. Nevertheless, with a little bit of luck the subject will have a good time.

Then, John Money and the Hampsons introduced the successful binary, sex and gender, in 1955 in their study of intersexed patients. They had a concept of a primary gender differentiation in which there is by the subject a self-designation as male or female, grounding the subject in a conviction that it is a biological female or male in accordance with assigned sex. But, a-signed sex is caused by an object thrown into the world. Still, there can't be much doubt that the boy and girl begin to diverge at the age of twelve months before the phallic phase, before the Oedipus, before, as it were, the anatomical sex distinction.

Stoller wanted to make this a little more precise with the concept of core gender identity. It does not seem accurate that the concept of core gender identity should fall under that of sex, the binary being male and female, being the biological dimension. Core gender identity is produced, he says, in the infant-parent relation, in the perception of the external genitalia and in a biological force.[17] The masculinity-femininity binary is an effect of identifications in the Oedipus and falls under the concept of just gender identity. Core gender identity is what is called in the discourse of philosophy essence, essence of femininity, of masculinity, even if Stoller mentions that any threats to it are threats to the subject's existence.[18]

It is rather a marvel that the subject by the age of twelve

months can consider itself a biological organism and self-designate as female or male, according to assigned sex. Sex is assigned in language. That is to say, it is gender from the beginning. We can eliminate the perception of external genitalia as a determinate of core gender identity since Stoller himself provides us with the case histories of two boys born without penises. They were accurately sexed and raised successfully as boys. It makes self-designation as a biological female or male just a little ambiguous. The body was sexed in a "symbiosis" with language in the infant-parent relation and not by perception of the external genitalia.

In an identification with pure signifiers sex is incorporated, according to Lacan,[19] but we cannot translate Lacan's *sexe* as the sex of sex and gender. The girl and the boy, the woman and the man are pure signifiers. Core gender identity is the effect of the relation of a speaking being to pure signifiers. If it is irreversible by the age of twelve months when the boy and the girl begin to diverge, that's because they have become signifiers. The overriding determinant of core gender identity is the way the parents speak to the subject. The subject could not designate itself as a biological entity such as male or female unless it were a speaking being. Indeed, in designating itself as male or female it is not designating itself as a biological entity at all but as a speaking being. Core gender identity is a function of language and does not fall under sex of the binary sex and gender. The signifiers are pure because they don't have a signified. They are signifiers waiting for their signified. Provided no foreclosure occurs, the signified arrives in the Oedipus.

Freud introduces sexual difference through pure signifiers in a naive remark which is supposedly a phenomenon between the comic and the joke. A three and half year old girl warns her brother not to eat too many sweets, that he will fall ill and have to take some "Bubizin" where "Bubi" is a boy. When she was ill, she took some "Medizin," where "Maedi" is a girl. "Medizin" is a medication for girls, and "Bubizin" a medication for boys. "Bubizin" is a pure signifier, a neologism in German. They are also gender terms, equivalent to masculine and feminine, for this subject.[20] Such signifiers are just as much operative at the moment of core gender identity.

These signifiers do not capture the essence of the girl or the boy. When the subject is captured by language, essence is lost. There is no essence of masculinity or femininity in the signifiers in play, no essence of the girl or boy in medication. The boy and the girl nevertheless exist thanks to a signifying system. These gender terms exist by virtue of language. Language supports existence and not essence. By supporting existence only and not essence, it does not support irreversibility but contingency. "Bubizin" as a gender term is not a logical necessity in the life of the sister or brother in the above scene.

It seems that sweets which are equal to an enjoyment plus an illness can be translated as *jouissance*. Then, the signifiers "Bubizin" and "Medizin" are meant to clear out this illness, evacuate this oral *jouissance*. The scene separates an erotic activity from gender roles. Gender is correlative to castration, defining castration as the signifier bringing a halt to *jouissance* which is the phallic signifier. John Money and his collaborators also ended up separating erotic activity from what he first called sex roles then gender roles or gender identity.

Gender is a psychologizing system and sexuation a logicising system. Gender is a system constructed out of a swamp of ideals jostling along side each other, whose order or disorder, with the exception of the transsexual, show themselves off in the field of the paternal metaphor which is logicised as All in the table of sexuation. Sexuation is an attempt to logicise the places of the man and the woman, and distributes "them two" between All and not-All on the connection and disconnection side of the table respectively. Between All and not-All and the gender binary, masculinity and femininity, there is some overlap but no one-one correspondence. We shall see that the disconnection side is putting a drain on any kind of essence that tries to emerge on the connection side.

Lacan's early remarks on gender, what he calls *sexe*, are bound up with the subject's existence. The Other is the place where the question of its existence is raised. The question concerns its gender. Am I a man or a woman? At this point in the evolution of his teaching the structure of neurosis is based on this question.[21] In 1958 the subject is divided over the question of gender: if the subject does not exist as a man or as a woman, it might not exist.[22] The subject is divided between existence and non-existence. He says there that gender is contingent and that the subject's existence is stupid and ineffable. It has to be sexed existence he is referring to. Existence as gendered subjects is stupid. In other words, there is already a latent orientation towards the disconnection-side. There couldn't be such an orientation were gender not contingent.

An orientation is something that has been brewing for a long time in his *Écrits*.[23] There is in *Encore* an orientation to the disconnection side of the table of sexuation where the woman is logicised as not-all. She is not-all in contrast to the connection side where the man is registered. As not-all she has a supplementary *jouissance* which has nothing to do with phallic *jouissance*. Had he considered the woman's *jouissance* as complementary to phallic *jouissance*, he says he would have made a mess and would have fallen back into the All.[24] The orientation in psychoanalysis is not to fall back into the All, that is, the orientation is to the not-All.

He says that language makes up for the sexual relation.[25] The unconscious as structured like a language is situated on the connection side of the table. The quantifier indicates that it is the side of the All, the universal, $\Phi$ indicates a sexed identification, a gender identification, with the phallus which is equivalent to $S_1$. The phallus is castration. The essence of the man is castration. But is it an essence? Probably not since he is not obliged to register himself here on this side. On the other hand, the woman is free to register herself on this side if it gives her pleasure. She makes this choice of sex anyway which is a choice of neurosis. The hysteric plays the part of the man. The phallus is a signifier that props the man up, but it is also propping her up. The phallus is a woman, and it is his symptom. There have always been phallic women.

On the disconnection side the negated universal indicates the not-All. Any speaking being, he says, can register on this side under the banner of women, whether this speaking being is provided with the attributes of masculinity or not. Attributes of masculinity are superfluous. In other words on the disconnection side the imaginary is excluded. One is a speaking being. The unconscious as structured like a language is situated on the connection side. A speaking being who registers itself on the disconnection side is disconnected from language. He remarks at the beginning of the Seminar that language is not the speaking being.[26] There is a speaking being for llanguage (*lalangue*) on the disconnection side.

Gender is derived from the Oedipus and has the paternal guarantee. Once that guarantee is withdrawn, gender disappears. The existential quantifier that heads the disconnection side indicates that the other sex is absent on this side. On the connection side traditional femininity jostles alongside traditional masculinity. What one calls sex is *heteros*, namely, the other sex.[27] Gender is operative on the connection side. There is no gender on the disconnection side. Femininity on the disconnection side is an experience, the experience of a supplementary *jouissance* whether one knows about it or not.

The sexual non-rapport creeps into language itself. By virtue of language there is an absent sexual relation. In *Encore* language makes up for the absent relation. In the following year's seminar he says that language is not a simple cork.[28] Or, to repeat myself, language does not create essence, by virtue of which the non-rapport is registered in language. Moreover, it seems that the connection side is being supported by the disconnection side: "What one calls sex…which is supported by the not-all, is strictly *heteros* which cannot shore itself up with the universal."[29] There is no heterosexuality on the disconnection side since there is no other sex. It cannot even shore itself up with the universal because language does not create essences.

Jacques-Alain Miller develops a logic of stratification to show how the not-all holds up the universal. Proposition 0 asserts the All outside of which therefore the Nothing. Proposition 8 asserts that Nothing is not all. Although the term sexuation and its table are not mentioned in the article, Propositions 0 and 8, show in "Matrix" that the logic of sexuation, of All and not-All, is the logic of stratification.[30] This is a key article in understanding why in "L'Étourdit" heteros is being held up by the not-All, and why gender cannot stem the tide with the universal.

Once again, Proposition 0 asserts the All outside of which therefore the Nothing. For my own peace of mind I will add that there cannot be outside the All. Therefore, a superior All must be asserted that includes them both. This is continued in Proposition 1 where each new All determines a Nothing, and again a superior All must be asserted. That is stratification. It is also repetition of the same All, and in Proposition 2 the nothing which is not-All is the cause of stratification or of the multiplication of the All. The not-All is holding up the heteros of the All in a logic of stratification. Proposition 4 asserts what appears to be a balance in the table of sexuation: the not-All does not cease to separate from the All, and the All does not cease to reabsorb the not-All—in my modification of a few terms. If that is supposed to represent some kind of balance in the table of sexuation, Proposition 10 makes it clear that it is precarious: the All and the not-All cannot be members of the same set. If that happens, there is unceasing disruption, the not-All robbing the All of any essence and the All robbing the not-All of its *jouissance*.

Finally, with only one signifier on the connection side, there is no reason to consider here an unconscious structured like a language. It is more like an unconscious as a way of enjoying the signifier which may not be, in effect, a connection-operator.

1. Lacan, Jacques, "L'Étourdit," *Scilicet* 4, Paris: Seuil, 1973.
2. Lacan, J., "The Signification of the Phallus" in *Écrits: A Selection*, London: Tavistock, 1977.
3. Lacan, J., *Le séminaire, Livre XXI: Les non-dupes errent*, unpublished.
4. *ibid*
5. Miller, Jacques-Alain, "Les six paradigmes de la jouissance," *La Cause freudienne* 43, Paris: 1999.
6. Lacan, J., *The Seminar, Book XX: On Feminine Sexuality, the Limits of Love and Knowledge: Encore*, NY: Norton, 1998.
7. *ibid*, p. 120.
8. *ibid*, p. 33.
9. Lacan, J., "D'une question préliminaire à tout traitement possible de la psychose," in *Écrits*, Paris: Seuil, 1966, p. 549.
10. *ibid*, p. 94.
11. *ibid*, p. 129, 131.
12. Lacan, J., *The Seminar, Book XX: On Feminine Sexuality, the Limits of Love and Knowledge: Encore*, NY: Norton, 1998. p. 33.
13. *ibid*
14. *ibid*, p. 35.
15. *ibid*
16. *ibid*, p. 5 and 7.
17. Stoller, Robert J., *Sex and Gender*, London: H. Karnac (Books) Ltd., 1984.
18. Essence is a debate that stretches from Antiquity to the present, and we might even be able to squeeze it into postmodernism.
19. op. cit., p. 39.
20. Freud, Sigmund, *Jokes and Their Relation to the Unconscious, S.E. VIII*, London: The Hogarth Press, 1986, p. 183.
21. Lacan, J., "D'une question préliminaire à tout traitement possible de la psychose," in *Écrits*, Paris: Seuil, 1966, p. 549.
22. *ibid*
23. Lacan, J., *The Seminar, Book XX: On Feminine Sexuality, the Limits of Love and Knowledge: Encore*, NY: Norton, 1998, p. 48.
24. *ibid*, p. 73.
25. *ibid*, p. 48.
26. *ibid*, p. 2.
27. Lacan, J., "L'Étourdit," *Scilicet* 4, Paris: Seuil, 1973, p. 23.
28. Lacan, J., *Le séminaire, Livre XXII: R.S.I.*, lecture 17 December 1974, *Ornicar?* 5.
29. Lacan, J., "L'Étourdit," *Scilicet* 4, Paris: Seuil, 1973, p. 23.
30. Miller, Jacques-Alain, "Matrix," *lacanian ink* 12, NY: Fall 1997. Original article in *Ornicar?* 4, Paris, 1975.

Jikta Hanzlová, "*Butterfly*", *Queens*, C-Print, 1999

# The Great Divide
## Psychoanalytic Contributions to the Diagnosis and Management of Psychosis*

Thomas Svolos

There are, of course, many diagnoses in the *DSM-4*,[1] various categories and gradations of psychopathology based on the clinical material—signs and symptoms—which can be easily and quickly grouped. This type of diagnostic system is best understood as a descriptive approach to nosology, where a diagnosis is based on easily observable or obtainable bits of information. In its modern form it is best attributed to Kraepelin and with the elaboration of the *DSM* has resulted in an expansive system of matrices and algorithms combining bits of information in a manner well suited for the dominant metaphor of our time, that of information technology. With the exception of the division between Axis 1 and Axis 2,[2] however, there are no major or essential distinctions among the diagnoses. Most American schools of psychoanalysis—ego psychology, object relations, and self psychology, which as a group I will henceforth term traditional psychoanalysis—have followed this categorization or descriptive nosological approach. Jacques Lacan and those adherent to the work of Freud as elaborated and expanded by Lacan, however, hold fast to a different orientation to the ques-

---

*Delivered at the University of Nebraska, Medical Center Department of Psychiatry, Grand Rounds, 12/01/1999

tion of diagnosis. For Lacanians, there are only three major diagnostic categories: that of psychosis, neurosis, and perversion. Given the relative rarity of perversion and the fact that the therapeutic approach to the patient with perversion is quite similar to that of neurosis, the key diagnostic issue becomes one of establishing whether the patient presents with psychosis.

Now: why would this seemingly archaic question of neurosis versus psychosis be important, especially to a clinician without interest in psychoanalysis—Lacanian or otherwise. After all, neurosis disappeared from standard psychiatric diagnoses in 1980 with the publication of the DSM-3.[3] There are two main reasons. The first is that the Lacanian theory of psychosis allows one to absolutely differentiate the presence or absence of psychosis, useful in situations where the clinician is unable to determine whether a "voice" represents a hallucination; or whether a particular disorganized thought process represents psychosis, or an acute hysterical crisis; or whether an odd or unusual thought represents a delusion; or whether the very sick and troubled patient before us—manifesting intense pathology—is extremely sick in a psychotic or non-psychotic manner. The importance of this degree of diagnostic precision, however, may not be immediately obvious. After all, a very sick patient, one might say, needs to be treated as a very sick patient and, well, voices are voices and the question may seem rather to be one of naming: are they psychotic versus non-psychotic hallucinations, or hallucinations versus perceptual abnormalities Not Otherwise Specified, perceptual abnormalities NOS, to use our current jargon? All of these distinctions, many would argue, are semantic and have no bearing on the clinical decisions—hospitalization, medication, type of therapy—we need to make in our approach to the patients. My second main assertion is that this is absolutely wrong. Our therapeutic approach to the patient must take a certain form—we must position ourselves to occupy a certain role or place in our work with psychotics—else we precipitate or exacerbate the psychosis and set up the conditions for a failure in treatment. Certain attitudes to take towards the patient, which may be necessary in the establishment of the transference in our work with neurotics—for example, taking a certain position or role of authority which physicians often do in dealing with patients—will be quite destructive in our relationships with psychotics.

Returning to diagnosis: diagnoses of the DSM are best thought of as syndromes—particular constellations of signs and symptoms, which the patient presents when certain criteria of duration, exclusion, and so forth are met—leading to the establishment of a particular diagnosis. The diagnosis is there—in all its presence—for all of us to see—on the surface of what can easily be observed or elicited through interview. This DSM diagnosis supposedly does not give a reason for the presentation—an etiology or mechanism—which would make of it an illness, and not a syndrome. Of course, many of us—most psychiatrists who use the DSM diagnostically—feel quite free to come forward with these explanations for the syndromes: the various theories of excesses or deficiencies in some substance or other which represent what has nicely been termed as the "neuromythology" of our profession, the expansion of one small scientific observation from biological psychiatry to an elaborate theory regarding how our psychopharmacologic agents work and the nature of the conditions which they treat. A careful reading of the psychiatric literature over time reveals the series of adoptions and rejections of one theory or another as the "reason" behind depression as an illness. None of this is meant to call into question the immense value of our psychopharmacologic arsenal for the control of symptoms, but to point out that the connection between empirically driven utility of these treatments does not correlate as nicely as one might think with specific etiologies for these syndromes. Someday, perhaps, as Freud once hoped and as Eric Kandel has advocated for, we will have such a unified field theory of the soul, of mental processes.[4] Certainly it behooves those of us caring for patients to be aware of developments in the biological sciences and science in general—Lacan was actually fascinated by math and science and commented throughout his career on the scientific nature and grounding for psychoanalysis. My assertion is that many of the discoveries of biological psychiatry have limited clinical relevance at our present time.

In trying to come to terms with the *DSM*, however, I think we need to recall Slavoj Zizek regarding the analysis of any discursive formation.[5] The truth of a discourse—discourse understood as a type of intellectual or cognitive formation, a symbolic system or structure, taken on by some institution—lies not in the overt self-representations of the discourse. In the case of the DSM its self-representation is an atheoretical system designed to facilitate communication between health care professionals. The truth is not found in the statements offered by the discourses themselves for why they are the way they are, the truth is found in the repressed history of the discourse, the past conflicts around the formation of the discourse. We tend to work, in fact, must work, with symbolic structures which define our knowledge—scientific understanding, political systems, systems of law, and so forth; we work with these as stable systems taken as "the way things are." However, when we investigate their past, their moment of emergence, it is often then that the true meaning behind the discourse emerges. The original *DSM* represented the combination of two separate needs—the needs of military psychologists to have a means to quickly categorize types of relatively minor pathology which might have significance in the wartime setting, and the needs of psychiatric hospitals to identify and track hospital censuses for epidemiological purposes. It was a document originally created not for use in clinical practice but to meet the requirements of the payees of the time, a function which it continues to fill quite well.

Lacanian diagnosis is based on a very different approach to the patient. Rather than identifying particular symptoms and signs which can be manipulated or combined into a syndromic construct—with its accompanying debate on etiologies for syndromes and what not—rather than such a descriptive, Kraepelinian nosology, psychoanalytic diagnosis is predicated on the encounter of the analyst with a certain discourse of the analysand, the patient. This discourse should be understood as something beyond the speech of the patient, to encompass speech and actions, and to this material must be added its negative, the unsaid, the words never spoken, or the failed speech—slips of the tongue and what not—and the similar negative actions of the patient, the late patient, the failure to pay, and so forth, all of which—in its full positive and negative valences—make up the discourse of what the patient presents to us. That matter of presentation to another, communication with another, is extremely important in that analysis is an intersubjective praxis.

Now, this discourse we are presented with, which we elicit in the questions (many or few) which we address to our patients, is structured in a certain manner, has a certain organization to it, has certain potential for meaning to it, has certain limits of communication as part of it—all based on the specificity of the structure itself. The structure (or, form, to use an older term from aesthetics) is the diagnosis, which, for Lacanians is limited to neurosis, psychosis, and perversion.

The structure, however, is not always immediately apparent in the discourse—the speech of the patient. The formal design of the discourse, though sometimes immediately apparent, can at other times take many sessions to be definitely identified.

Identification of perversion in the establishment of a diagnosis is not nearly so important in the early approach to working with a patient as is identification of psychosis because much of the technique used in working patients with perversion is similar to that of working with neurotics, especially in the early stages. Furthermore, failure to identify perversion does not result in the complications which are seen in failing to identify psychosis. The key question, diagnostically, which must be reiterated until answered definitively, has to do with psychosis.[6]

In the interview with the neurotic patient, what one is looking for, diagnostically, are signs of the unconscious. Unlike psychosis, in which we might say that the unconscious does not exist, neurosis is defined by the presence of the unconscious. There are many signs which might indicate its presence, perhaps the most classic of which are the discursive features identified by Freud as the material of analysis, the aspects of the analysand's discourse which attract our attention, namely: dreams, slips of the tongue, parapraxes (or bungled actions), and jokes. In our usual conversation with one another, including that with patients, the speaking subject feels in control of his words—he says what he wants to say, thinks what he wants to think, and delivers a message which he feels can be understood by the others with whom he is speaking. The unconscious, however, manifests itself as an extreme disruption. In the midst, say, of an explanation of some historical fact of a patient's life, there will be a slip of the tongue. The patient may not notice it or deny any significance to it. That slip is a glimpse of the unconscious, a demonstration that the contents of the unconscious want to make themselves known. If the ego of the patient refuses to speak the unconscious, the subject will, however, speak itself in the interstices of the discourse. Dreams as well, in as much as they often seem bizarre, seem disturbing, with—again—glimpses of truth that are often refused or denied, similarly are signs of the unconscious, and jokes as well with similar characteristics of—often—a disturbing, bizarre, or disruptive nature—certainly something we wouldn't be saying with a straight face, something that can only be said through the joke—and I would emphasize that exact sense of words. It is not that I can only say this through a joke, but something that can only be said through a joke. That thing, a seemingly foreign object—repulsive, bizarre, disturbing—is the unconscious.

These discursive formations are not the only signs, symptoms themselves exist as manifestations of the unconscious. A neurotic will present to the doctor or therapist a symptom—sometimes vague such as a lack of energy, or depression or nervousness, sometimes more specific such as impotence but nonetheless something recognizable as a symptom. Again, something disturbing, unexplainable, perhaps, bizarre, often something felt as alien and, again, something about which the patient has doubts and for which an explanation may be demanded. That symptom as well takes the form as a sign of the unconscious.

If there is a unifying feature to all of these phenomena—dreams, jokes, slips, symptoms—it is that of their form. They are all, in fact, notable as disturbances, irregularities, which upset the smooth, steady functioning we think we have as we go about our daily business, or nightly business, in the case of sleep. And, as Freud showed us in what certainly must be his most critical discovery, their existence as phenomena is quite remarkable. In fact, at some level it is useful to think of these phenomena as non-existent. They exist only as disturbances in the form of our speech, acts and what not and they are best thought of in negative terms—failures and misconnections of discourse communication. The key point, however, is that they are not random events, trivial errors, or insignificant anomalies. They are signs that refer to the existence of another place—the unconscious—which can only be perceived or glanced at through these negative forms. What Freud did was show that there is meaning to these random, trivial, and insignificant events, and that that meaning is localized to what he named the unconscious. A site of meaning radically different from our ordinary meaning, a site of meanings—or better yet simply thoughts—that neurotic subjects want to know nothing of, thoughts that, because of pain or some other reason, were put away for good, placed into recesses of the mind and carefully kept there. This is repression. Repression does not exist, however, independent of its return. In as much as a certain function of the ego might be to censor these thoughts and keep them out of consciousness, they are constantly striving to re-express themselves in discourse and do that in precisely the form of dreams, jokes, and so forth. One of the significant aspects of the analysis of neurotics is the use of interpretation to gain access to these unconscious thoughts. Thus, in working with neurotics—both in diagnosis and later treatment—the parts of discourse which the analyst is focusing on are precisely these formal irregularities—disturbances of dreams, jokes, slips and symptoms. Repression and the return of the repressed thoughts in distorted phenomena is the proper form of neurosis.

For any given neurotic, repression is understood as a result of an encounter with what is called *le Nom-du-Père*. Unlike traditional psychoanalysis with its complicated and somewhat disorienting division into oral, anal, phallic, latent, and genital stages of development, Lacan based his theory on the more fundamental and significant issue of the acquisition of or incorporation into language. This is what clearly distinguishes man from other beings of nature, the way in which language is taken on or incorporated by the subject is the most significant fact of existence. Traditional psychoanalysis attempts to investigate, structure and recover the pre-language era of the subject. The task is doomed to failure because of the lack of memory at that developmental age, because, of course, there is no memory of that time or even at that time. We could even more radically state that the subject does not even exist at that time, prior to the development of language, logic and memory. It is not that that time is repressed, for repression implies a registering or coding of perceptions and sensations and a subsequent censoring from consciousness. The pre-language era is a developmental era when such a registering does not even occur. Our best efforts to attempt to understand this pre-language state are thus only very partial. We can hypothesize that what might be involved at that time is a lack of boundary between the subject and the environment around him, a type of immediate response to internal and external stimuli as pleasurable and painful, and the specifically human absolute state of dependence on the Mother, our strongly altricial state which is a function of our species' use of language itself. Thus, the Mother is the function of providing basic care that could be done by the actual mother or father or any other person or combination not necessarily related to the person. The choice of the word Mother for this function is an acknowledgment of a certain typical assignment of that role in our modern Western family structure.

What we like to call now developmental window, this dyadic relationship between the child and the Mother is broken up and the name for that function—the function that severs the intimate Mother-Child dyad—is *le Nom-du-Père*. The words themselves translate as both Name of the Father and Noun of the Father, but this is a homonym as well for No-of-the-Father. And again, the function of the Father, while traditionally identified with the actual Father in our modern Western family structure, might also be filled by the mother (who may even fill both functions in a single parent family), but also other bodies representing authority, such as the Judge or Law or the Church or a Nation. In any case, the initial happening is that a "No!" is articulated, the No-of-the-Father separating the child from the Mother in what Lacan terms alienation. The immediate connection with the Mother, the sense of oneness with the Mother is severed and the subject loses a certain connection with its enjoyment and pleasure in as much as that was immediately provided by the Mother. A certain sexualized bond between the child and mother is lost. The second stage is termed separation, where the Name-of-the-Father comes to name the desire of the Mother. To put this in psychological terms: the child has lost something and is at a loss as to what that is and takes the desire of the Mother for the Father, for that thing that separated them, as its own. This paternal metaphor, or naming of the mother's desire as the Father, is the basis for all the metaphoric substitutions which make up the language of neurosis. This process leads to and is in fact synonymous with repression. Precisely that which happens when the child is forced to give up that special relationship with the mother and the trauma of that sacrifice, what Freud also termed castration, is the kernel of the repressed. Thus, everything which we identified as specific to the discourse of neurotics—

dreams, slips of the tongue, and so forth—is tied to this encounter with *le Nom-du-Père*.

To state the fact of psychosis most succinctly: this encounter with *le Nom-du-Père* does not happen. It fails. Instead of having an acknowledgment of the No of the Father and a successful separation of the child from the Mother and a Naming of desire, in psychosis, *le Nom-du-Père* is foreclosed, refused, and pushed out of existence by the subject as if it never existed in the first place. It is not repressed. It is not even registered. It is removed from the field. The psychotic subject, of course, takes on language, learns language and can communicate with language, but in a different manner, for in psychosis—without an acknowledgment, though repressed, of *le Nom-du-Père*, without separation from the mother and establishment of the paternal metaphor—there is no unconscious. Psychotic patients do not have an unconscious. Now what does that mean to state there is no unconscious? To start with, there can be no signs of the presence of the unconscious. This is one way to identify psychosis as based on the lack of properly neurotic phenomena. For example, it is extraordinarily rare for a psychotic to have a slip of the tongue. I have never seen a psychotic patient report the type of parapraxis or bungled action that neurotic patients frequently report. With regard to dreams, the situation is somewhat different, for psychotic patients do, of course, dream. The interesting thing about this has to do with the character of and reception to their dreams that psychotic patients make. I have spent much time with psychotics asking about dreams and it is fairly rare that psychotic patients will remember and produce their dreams for sessions. Furthermore, the dreams often have an extraordinarily matter-of-fact character to them. In general, ironically, I find them to be often less bizarre than those of neurotics. The subject matter of the dream is often straightforward. Finally, they are only quite rarely received with interest. Psychotics have no curiosity about the dreams, unlike even the most obsessional neurotic patient who over time will develop an interest in dreams.

And if any interpretation by the patient begins with respect to his dream, it is marked with a great deal of certainty—for example that such a symbol must represent something else. This is quite different from neurotics, whose interpretations of dreams tend to be marked by a great deal of ambiguity and doubt.

There are some features of the psychotic language, however, which can be picked up in an initial interview. The first of these has to do with certainty. The language of the neurotic is, in general, marked by a series of doubts, hesitancies, and indecisions. There is stumbling, there can be retractions and all sorts of failings. Even the most rigid obsessional neurotic will, as interviews progress, begin to break down in his attempts at absolute control over his language. All of this is reflective of a certain ambiguous state with regard to meaning—as it can be expressed in communication—and is a sort of tacit acknowledgment of the existence of the unconscious. The psychotic's discourse, however, is rich in certainty. That is not to say that a psychotic patient cannot have doubt, but that the basis of the doubt is in a degree of certainty. If we take a question of perception—a hallucination—and try to understand this within standard psychiatric constructs, we can quite quickly be stuck in a great muddle. For example, we know that so-called normal people will, under a situation of sleep deprivation, see things—have perceptions—which are not grounded in reality. Furthermore, many patients—notoriously hysterical neurotics (or what some now call borderlines in micro-psychotic breaks)—who are fundamentally not psychotic have hallucinations as part of their symptomatology. The question again is what are we to call these? And, more importantly, in the situation of an interview where a seemingly odd perception is reported, to what extreme do we have to go to determine whether this is reality-based or not, a task extraordinarily difficult in most cases. The more interesting thing to observe is not whether a patient quickly acknowledges the presence or absence of voices and moves on to the next symptom on the checklist. The more interesting thing is to listen to the patient talk about his experience, for the certainty of the meaning given to the experience is the key to determining whether this is psychotic. Lacan states in his Seminar III:

> Reality is not the issue. The subject admits, by means of all the verbally expressed detours at his disposal, that these phenomena are of another order than the real. He is well aware that their reality is uncertain. He even admits their unreality up to a certain point. But, contrary to the normal subject for whom reality is always in the right place, he is certain of something, which is that what is at issue—ranging from hallucination to interpretation—regards him. Thus, while doubt may exist at the perceptual level, there is a certainty of meaning specific to psychosis. Reality isn't at issue for him, certainty is. Even when he expresses himself along the lines of saying that what he experiences is not of the order of reality, this does not affect his certainty that it concerns him. The certainty is radical. The very nature of what he is certain of can quite easily remain completely ambiguous, covering the entire range from malevolence to benevolence. But it means something unshakable for him. This constitutes what is called, whether rightly or wrongly, the elementary phenomenon or, as a more developed phenomenon, delusional belief.[7]

Thus, while doubt may exist at the perceptual level, there is a certainty of meaning specific to psychosis.

Another aspect of language disturbance specific to psychosis and, at times, seen in diagnostic interviews is the neologism. In this case, there is a novel symbolic construct, a new association or group of phonemes (syllables) which are placed together. Now, the interesting thing is a certain similarity between some types of slips of the tongue, which are constructed of phonemes often, and neologisms. When the neurotic produces a slip of the tongue, we quickly understand it as such because of the meaning given to it by the neurotic. Either its enunciation is denied, or if acknowledged and meaning given to it, is of diminished importance as "simply" being a slip of the tongue and thus without meaning. The neologism may—on paper, taken out of context—appear no different from a slip. The key difference is the meaning given to it. The psychotic associates a great deal of intentionality to its utterance and often makes of it a word quite rich in meaning.

The dialectic of meaning itself is quite specific in psychosis. With the neurotic, words are strung together to create phrases and sentences which have meanings and this creation involves often a metaphoric process through which the neurotic acknowledges a certain distance to meaning or a certain failure to have meaning itself and an acknowledgment that this stringing together of words only partly achieves its function. The psychotic, on the other hand, does not seem to be able to achieve the appropriate level of distance from meaning to generate it in the usual metaphorical, neurotic manner (recall there is no normal here). A certain degree of looseness with respect to words is necessary to produce metaphoric meaning. The psychotic cannot do this, having never installed the paternal metaphor in the first place, and is left with two possible relationships to meaning. The first is the overly close association of meaning to a word, what psychiatrists commonly refer to as concreteness. A patient is frequently called concrete if he is too insistent on meanings being tied to specific words, regardless of the context. This concreteness ultimately leads to a certain failure in meaning as the concrete psychotic is unable to handle the implied and assumed meanings of speech. The opposite problem in this regard is so-called looseness of associations in all of its forms—from circumstantiality to flight of ideas—where the stringing together of words is so seemingly random that meaning too is lost. All this alludes to the failure of metaphor in the psychotic patient. I would here incidentally note the resulting improper terminology of looseness of associations. Neurotic speech is based on a certain looseness of associations, a certain play of words, without which we would speak concretely. Looseness is itself part of metaphoric speech. The danger is not looseness per se but excessive looseness.

For the analysis of neurotics to proceed, even in successful non-analytic therapeutic relationships, the progress of the work is based on a certain transference building from the patient to the analyst. The patient comes to believe in the analyst as someone who knows something—an authority—and often as someone who takes on the role of an authoritative figure from the past of the subject. This transference relationship is the motor force of the analysis of neurotics, what makes it work. With psychotics, allowing such a transference to develop can have devastating consequences, inducing a first overt psychotic break (with hallucinations and delusions) or worsening psychotic symptoms in a patient.

These clinical structures, such as neurosis and psychosis, are present beginning at the age of the acquisition of language and remain throughout life. Thus, all of these psychotic patients are psychotic from childhood on. Our psychiatric experience supports this, for example in the retroactively identifiable prodromal period of schizophrenia, or, more interestingly, in the future schizophrenics which researchers have been able to identify blindly in watching videos of patients and their cohorts. In previous times in psychiatry, there were terms such as latent schizophrenia for this. Lacanian analysts adopt precisely the term pre-psychotic for just such a subject—child or adult—who may have never had a psychotic break with the proliferation of all the Schneiderian first-rank symptoms, but who has foreclosed *le Nom-du-Père* and thus has psychotic language use as detailed above, language use whose peculiarities are recognized in the cognitive dimension of psychosis now popular in psychiatric research. In any case, these pre-psychotics may under certain conditions be triggered into a psychosis. The condition that causes this is precisely an encounter with *le Nom-du-Père* which occurs too late. In other words, if a psychotic patient—after the phase of language acquisition—encounters a person or institution who attempts to take a symbolic role of authority, or calls the patient to a certain symbolic role, or names that which the pre-psychotic must desire, that is, if a psychotic encounters the roles or functions of *le Nom-du-Père*, then that encounter can precisely trigger a psychotic break. In our most famous case of psychosis—that of Judge Schreber[8]—it is the encounter with the symbolic role of the Judge in an appointment to an elite Supreme Court position, and the encounter with the role of a Father that triggered his break. Above all else, in our dealings with psychotics or suspected psychotics, we must ensure that we do not position ourselves in this role of authority, as this *Nom-du-Père*. Even in the case of patients who have entered into an acutely psychotic phase or whose psychosis has stabilized, this matter of how one positions oneself continues to be very important. Any positioning of the analyst or therapist in certain authority roles—roles which all of our neurotic patients make of us and we ourselves are only too happy to assume—can lead to the establishment of a strongly negative relationship of the psychotic patient to the doctor which can lead to breaking of the therapeutic relationship, worsening of psychotic symptoms or frank defiance of the treatment plan.

What is the treatment goal for psychotics? Within a diagnostic system based on the presence and combinations of symptoms which constitute a syndrome, symptom alleviation certainly becomes a focus of therapy, be they so-called positive, negative or cognitive symptoms. Our experience with pharmacotherapy shows us that we can be somewhat effective in treating some positive symptoms and we may have moderate effects on negative symptoms and cognition. I would like to briefly examine one part of this—the treatment of delusions. Delusional disorder, previously known as paranoia, is, we know, quite resistant to pharmacotherapy and when treating schizophrenics, we know that hallucinations are much easier to control than delusions. Furthermore, in terms of prognosis, we know that psychotic patients with delusional disorder have often higher functioning than those with schizophrenia and that within the range of schizophrenic subtypes, those with paranoid, or delusional, schizophrenia, have the best prognosis.

Finally, delusions are protective against violence on the part of psychotic patients, one of our great concerns in working with psychotics.[9] I bring forth all of these psychiatric observations as evidence supporting the psychoanalytic theory that delusions, what Lacan calls the delusional metaphor, are in a way not part of the psychosis itself, but rather the psychotic subject's solution to the psychosis. Without the installation of the paternal metaphor, everything regarding meaning—the language forms specific to psychosis—is quite unstable for the psychotic. The delusional metaphor is evolved as a substitute for the paternal metaphor and by distributing meaning across the language and the world of the psychotic, the delusional metaphor can lead to a certain stability and sense of peace of the psychotic patient, however bizarre and untrue we may find the system. To close off exploration or evolution of a delusional system in our interview or therapy with patients may disable them from ever finding peace in the world.

As a final note on treatment, I wish to refer to treatment planning. This process is one I have observed most doctors are bored with, seeing it as the role of the various so-called ancillary providers. For psychotic patients, I think our active participation is crucial, on both inpatient and outpatient levels. We see the patients on a regular basis and should have a good sense of their degree of stress or tension in their interaction with the different communities they are involved with, be they family, group home, day program, job or whatever. And we can play an important role in assessing the level of symptoms progressively over time. Our overall management of the case involves knowing all of this and establishing a treatment plan appropriate for the patient, for just as an authoritative physician may lead to all sorts of deterioration, an overly authoritative or directive treatment plan may have the exact same results. Community integration, a laudable possible goal for patients, should not be seen as the ultimate goal for all psychotics. As we have seen, certain symbolic roles—sometimes something as seemingly simple as being an employee, or having an apartment—can in fact lead to similar psychotic deterioration and we must play a vital role in ensuring that some other institution's goals do not interfere with what is in the best interests of the patient.

1. American Psychiatric Association, *Diagnostic and Statistical Manual of Mental Disorders IV,* Washington, DC: APA, 1994.
2. In the *DSM*, Axis 1 disorders represent clinical disorders and Axis 2 disorders are personality disorders.
3. American Psychiatric Association, *Diagnostic and Statistical Manual of Mental Disorders III,* Washington, DC: APA, 1980.
4. Kandel, Eric R., "A New Intellectual Framework for Psychiatry," in *American Journal of Psychiatry* 155, 04/98 and "Biology and the Future of Psychoanalysis: A New Intellectual Framework for Psychiatry Revisited," in *American Journal of Psychiatry* 156, 04/99. Freud's enthusiasm for such a possibility in his Project [Freud, Sigmund, *Project for a Scientific Psychology, S. E. I,* London: Hogarth Press, 1966] is somewhat subdued later into his psychoanalytic career [Freud, S., *On Narcissism: An Introduction, S. E. XIV*].
5. Zizek, Slavoj, *Tarrying the Negative: Kant, Hegel, and the Critique of Ideology,* Durham: Duke Univ. Press, 1993.
6. Lacan, Jacques, "On a Question Preliminary to any Possible Treatment of Psychosis," in *Écrits: A Selection,* NY: Norton, 1977, and *The Seminar, Book III: The Psychoses,* NY: Norton, 1993.
7. *ibid*, p. 75.
8. Schreber, Daniel Paul, *Memoirs of My Nervous Illness,* Cambridge: Harvard Univ. Press, 1988.
9. Applebaum, Paul S. et al., "Violence and Delusions: Data From the MacArthur Violence Risk Assessment Study," in *American Journal of Psychiatry* 157, 04/00.

# The Absence of the 20th Century

GÉRARD WACJMAN

translated by JORGE JAUREGUI

Since the dawn of the last century, art has been directed by a basic movement, which can be traced to Duchamp and Malevich. From this perspective I approach Jochen Gerz, an artist of the late 20th century. An artist at the end. I will discuss three works in his oeuvre which illuminate an essential aspect of this past century. The hidden face of the 20th century.

1

To say that Jochen Gerz is an "artist," may need some clarification. An "artist" that does not draw, does not paint, and does not sculpt. He passes his time speaking on the telephone, answering the mail, surfing the net, sending faxes and things of this sort. He is not preoccupied with beauty, he does not create objects in the usual sense. He does not make art in the way we habitually assume. Nevertheless Gerz is an artist. Modern? It's called "conceptual."

Like all authentic works, his is exceptional and asserts itself by way of its very exceptionalness.

This seems so evident that, at first sight—and first wonder—his work appears to run counter to what I would propound as the prevailing movement in modern art. Thus these art works evince an unequivocal rapport to the signifier, or to symbols: monuments. One way or the other, every monument is a monument to the social order; in any case, monuments bear on the signifier of power since they are tied to a public commissions. For Gerz, funding has come from the Saarland, the cities of Hamburg and Bremen, the town hall at Biron, a charming village in Dordogne, etc.

These curious monuments, they certainly exist, yet the essence of their subject matter remains somehow tricky to define. Like all monuments they deal with memory, yet it is as if, on their behalf, you must take literally the proposal "making work by memory." Their subject matter is memory, much as others erect edifices in concrete or in iron.

Finally, a last curiosity, but not least, these works do not call upon an a priori debate on resemblance, because, apart from them not resembling works of art, they essentially—each in its own way—put forward nothing to see.

2

Thus three monuments: *Das Hamburger Mahnmal gegen Faschismus*, the Anti-Fascist Memorial in Hamburg, in collaboration with Esther Shalev-Gerz, unveiled in October 1986. *2146 Steine-Mahnmal gegen Rassismus, Saarbrücken*, 2146 Stones-Monument against Racism in Saarbrücken, 1993. *Le monument vivant de Biron*, The Living Monument of Biron, France, 1996.

Three brief descriptions:

The Anti-Fascist Memorial: Built in suburban Hamburg, a large seaport severely damaged during WW II, it was inaugurated in 1986. A square cut column, 40 feet high (the average height of the city's buildings) by 3 feet wide on each of its four sides, it was entirely wrapped with sheets of blank lead. A *modus operandi* in eight different languages, fixed to the a nearby wall, invited bystanders to leave their signatures on the monument by carving their names in the lead with the aid of stilettos provided for the occasion (some, by night, left their mark with straight gunshots). In addition, the column was meant to gradually sink into the ground, approximately 6 feet every year; so that in November 1993, six years later, the column had completely vanished into the ground, gone, its flat top alone appearing at the street level. All you can see is some sort of paving stone. A first phase of the monument has thus been achieved: Gerz says that the monument "has changed its identity."[1] The *modus operandi* thoroughly explains the rationale behind its sinking and vanishing. The last phase is: "Since nothing can stand up for us against injustice."

2146 Stones-Monument against Racism: Saarbrücken, a German town not far from the French border. An alley in the city center leads to the castle—now the seat of the Parliament of the Saar—where the Gestapo had its headquarters during WW II. The alley, about 800 feet long, is made of 8,000 paving stones, of which Jochen Gerz picked 2146 at random. The figure corresponds to the number of Jewish cemeteries existing in Germany prior to 1939.[2] The 2146 cobblestones were engraved with the name of one of the cemeteries, and then reinstated in the alley, and sealed, the inscribed side facing the ground. So that, after lengthy labor, the alley's appearance was complete unchanged. Since Gerz disposed of the planting map, no one knows where the engraved cobblestones lie. Its induction in 1993 consisted of unveiling a new street plate: the "Square of the Castle" officially became the "Square of the Invisible Monument." It's the only visible trace of this Monument against Racism.[3]

The Living Monument of Biron: Commissioned by the Municipality of Biron in Dordogne (and by the French Ministry of Culture) to replace the village War Memorial, timeworn and deteriorated, dating from 1921. With its obelisk, the monument was modelled on the commonest of French War Memorials. Jochen Gerz expressly carved the exact same monolith, cut from local rock, except that this one is new. An exact copy, although without the cracks, of course. In the Spring of 1996, over fifteen days, he interviewed each one of the 127 inhabitants of the *commune*, asking them an alleged "secret question." Each answer was engraved on a small red enamelled plate, which were affixed randomly to the newly carved War Memorial. Chiefly the texts speak about death and war, but also about peace and other things. It says: "Before, the war of others was faraway, nowadays it's near," "It's worth while to risk your own life for your country," "I was stationed in Guinea for three years and saw comrades meet with foul play. War is not appealing."

### 3

In Gerz's three works there is nothing to see, albeit in an unusual way.[4] We are thus deprived of a long aesthetic debate, although we mat examine this "invisibility," inquire into its causes, reflect upon its meaning, derive an assorted variety of readings. Every explanation is not necessarily true, each one conveys a different value.

You could, for instance, consider the comment from James Young, who speaks of "anti-monuments;" or one of Gerz own remarks: "I made them because I don't like monuments."[5] Militant iconoclast! *Agent provocateur* against the Establishment. Contesting interpretation? These are irresolute constructions.

You may, by way of a slight *bricolage* set your sights higher and rank the work of Jochen Gerz within the category Yves Michaud calls "art to which we don't pay attention." A sort of art by no means deficient, cosmetic or lacking innovation, but an art that, in the 20th century, opposes big paintings and the *imagines symbolicae* with a "more lateral" gaze. Art would be effecting a sort of displacement that consists in conveying to the center of perception what is usually in the margins. Indeed, Yves Michaud ponders whether "it wouldn't be excessive to state that the 20th century witnessed the passage from an art you look at to one where somehow there's nothing to see."[6] It's not an exaggeration to say this is the case as far as Gerz's works. The nothing-to-see peculiar to these monuments against Fascism or against Racism seems of a different sort than the stains, colorings, rippings, etc., all this kind of nothing-to-see of painting.

4

To cut short possible misunderstanding, I will argue on behalf of what I term the modern rupture. Here, invisibility entails an absolute clause of disengagement from mimesis, the zenith of non-resemblance, the achievement of imaginary ripping. Gerz as the modern, radical and consequential artist.

Inasmuch as Gerz follows the non-representational aesthetic debate in Claude Lanzmann's *Shoah*, the explanatory register has its coherence.[7] Nonetheless it seems to me that *Shoah*'s aesthetic contention, certainly bound to cinema and to a specific theme, is saddled with an issue, like the dark stripe of the zebra, that stigmatizes all art produced today: all represented bodies, all figures, all faces, in fact, any image or form today is marked in some way by the battered bodies of Auschwitz[8] Regarding the art of the second half of the century, gas chambers constitute a sort of fossilized vibration rumbling behind every work, beyond all matters of gender, subject matter or style.[9] As if Catastrophe were art's ultimate referent in this fin de siècle.

After all, Adorno conceivably fell shy when he declared the impossibility of poetry in the aftermath of Auschwitz (or, as I suggested in the beginning, it may be peremptory to dissociate art and poetry in this respect). It doesn't seem extravagant nor useless to put forth the question, simply, whether art indeed changed after the gaz chambers, and how. Just the assumption that this could

# The Absence of the 20th Century

JOCHEN GERZ, *2146 Stones-Monument against Racism*, 1990-93

have made an imprint, through diverse forms, by an acceleration of imaginary deflation, a pronounced fracture of resemblance.[10] The image of an agonized body, and, from there, all the images.

This would require stretching Adorno's thought, and thus contradicting it: if impossibility exists in art, then it must be combined with necessity. Far from calling from theories about the end of art, art, on the contrary, has appeared in its absolute in its absolute necessity: as that which aims at the impossible.

5

Consequently, since Gerz work, against all misreading, has taken this particular "issue" as object, I see a certain benefit (and, I must acknowledge, I derive a certain malicious pleasure) in directing reflection to another speculative course, and one that goes precisely counter to commentary up until now as concerns the link between modernity and the deficiency of resemblance. What if instead of functioning as a radical rupture vis-à-vis mimesis, the nothing-to-see in Gerz's monuments were here semblance itself, its most faithful way, the most accurate to figure out the matter in hand, the loudest cry of truth?"

And there is an unexpected angle to consider. What if Gerz, within a hyper-modern conceptual gloss, is really a classic artist? It all depends on one question: what can these works depict best, what object is to be represented? The case is not that because there is nothing to see, there is nothing it resembles, but to pose the question inversely: to what object that, by definition, one does not see, do these works resemble well, trait for trait, to the point of constituting true portrait?

Here is in any case an artist who obliges mental gymnastics if you are to inquire what might be the object whose faithful portrait is invisible. And from there: what is necessary for this object's existence, what degree of sophistication should the notion of object have to lay claim to an invisible work being its true representation?

# The Absence of the 20th Century 67

Jochen Gerz is a portraitist, why not? The label is easily met: he himself alludes to the dimension of resemblance apropos The Anti-Fascist Memorial in Hamburg. "The work," he says, "is addressed to all people who have said: 'We saw nothing, we weren't there.' To them the object 'answers:' 'I'm not there either.' It's up to them to reclaim it. Like the past they keep denying. It's a game of mimesis. Art is dressed as a spectator."[11]

Here, precisely here, the case is not the absence of object in the conceptual terms of an art without object, as a "work of art constricted to its enunciate function." It is meant differently. Art is not casually disjointed from the object, it necessarily so; for art to exist, it must be disjointed from all objects of art. To fabricate an art object in the guise of a monument is to fabricate an excuse. Thus here, precisely here, art should speak up and refuse to become an excuse. And this is why Jochen Gerz does not fabricate an object here, but on the contrary he withdraws it. In order to make art.

You may gauge the optimistic violence that The Anti-Fascist Memorial exerts upon onlookers, and how it offsets the traditional purpose of the monument, which is supposed to function as a social mobilizer, to congregate in the communion of memory. All commemoration leads to communion, always more or less religious. Yet Gerz's monuments run counter to the celebratory mood. In lieu of endorsing an "official" memory, of perpetuating present recollections, they reveal something else; they unveil and show what is: oblivion. They set up an other memory. An unexpected Other recalls the memory of the City. At once the monuments do not prompt togetherness, they foster division. These invisible monuments have a peculiar power to exhibiting what you are not suppose to see.

These works "make you see." To be rigorous, saying that they "to make see" is not the same as saying that they are "visible;" strictly speaking these works do not render anything "visible." The character of these "invisible" works by Gerz consists precisely in making the "visible" arise where it is lacking, to exhibit the absence of bodies and memory gaps that keep out the perceptible space we call reality. In this, Gerz's conceptual monuments are by no means equivalents of discourse, they are visual works-of-the-art precisely because their character is not "to say" but to reinsert what cannot be said, the absent, in the field of the visible. Moreover, one could even say that The Anti-Fascist Memorial in Hamburg "renders visible" to the letter: the signatures engraved in the metal or the holes from the gunshots. Finally, the memorial makes a space for the presence of the witnesses, and creates a physical depression in the form of their closed eyes.

After this presentation, I believe you may better understand Gerz, and more fully than as a provocative sally, as if Gerz pretends to make monuments because he doesn't like them. Every monument conveys time and memory into the social space. Let's say that a monument functions as a bank deposit, as a frozen account in the social memory. In this way it contributes toward repression, which it favours and lauds, as if it were a night watchman of old who roamed the streets calling "sleep well good people," all monuments say to city dwellers "You all forget, I remember!"

What else do war memorials in provincial townships say? Other than an unattractiveness close to kitsch, most of the time, monuments are no longer pay much attention. As Gerz says: "Memory is like blood, it's fine as long as we don't see it." That's the problem with monuments.

It is exactly this which seems "to mime" or "to say" the fact that Gerz has, in place of the old War Memorial in Biron which you couldn't see anymore, erected a copy that mirrored the preceding one. The new monument, by definition, you cannot see either, "except " for the shingled red plates with words fixed on top, these "show" that it is there, and that you do not see it. Surprisingly the original stone memorial has become the bedrock of the new "monument," which is reduced to the written text. The obelisk is "visible" in the same way that the background is "visible" on a sheet of paper covered with writing. It could be said that the marks "repress" the background. A small operation, which needs to be reassessed in this light: the "secret question" the viewers are asked by Gerz is a catalyst for the memory of the villagers,

JOCHEN GERZ, study for *The Living Monument*, 1995/96

activating memory, awakening memory over war and death. It suffices to read the given answers,[12] which are, of course, far from being entirely pacifistic. As Gerz says: "remembrance is a contemporary act. This is to say that The Living Monument of Biron deserves its name: bedecked with red plates, it is devoted to the dead, it stands in the central village marketplace as a living objection to death.[13] A Monument that says: "Death to death!"

6

But if we look close enough, what exactly does Gerz's work consist of? And what is a real monument? It is not the obelisk in the central market, not really the red plates with villagers' words: it's the inhabitants themselves. It's "them" that by dint of "the secret question" are the bearers of memory. They may also, when explaining the meaning of this bizarre War Memorial to their children, tell them with a flushed face as if sickened with measles, about their coming to Biron in 1996, of a rather bizarre German artist who instead of carving stones, asked them a bizarre question about their thoughts on war and death. "Art is dressed as a spectator," and the spectators are dressed like monuments. The title itself is to be taken literally, no metaphor here: the monument "is" alive.

I myself, when commenting on the work, have the feeling of being part of this "monument." I detect Gerz cancelling the gap between three fundamental elements: the work, the author and the viewer (a divisive and opposing perspective, which art since the Renaissance has tried to encompass).

It's as though Gerz's monumental work has performed a transfer of memory, conveying the dead recollections of monuments, which mortify memory, into the viewer's living memory. This task melts away petrified memories—remember spring is not always laughing.

## 7

When we consider The Monument against Racism at Saarbrücken, another aspect comes to the fore.[14] The danger today, apropos Shoah, is that in Europe memory is reabsorbed in an irresistible patrimonial frenzy, hastening the way to the Great Commemoration. It is alarming that Holocausts museums are being concocted here and there. Museums are places where memory turns into History, much as it gets petrified in the objects. Broadly speaking, the danger[15] is in the monuments, in monumentalizing. The cobblestones with the engraved names of the Jewish cemeteries existing during the Third Reich that Gerz cloaked underground hamper the commemorative and petrifying mood. The Saarbrücken monument is not a souvenir memorial but a memorial to holes in the memory, a memorial to oblivion, loss, absence, to the actual facts—like the memories, oblivion is a contemporary act. The "Invisible Monument" is not recalled by past facts: it is obliteration, always in the present, the fact of which there is no substantial record, nowhere, nor recollection whatsoever of the Jewish life that existed in Germany in 39 years ago, at least, in the 2146 communities (which one can conclude from the existence of 2146 cemeteries). The cemeteries themselves are memory recalls. Gerz created a monument that recalls oblivion and beyond oblivion: the vanishing of proper traits, of memory's fossilized remains in the guise of burial stones.

The Saarbrücken monument is neither pretty nor therapeutic, and it doesn't oblige the work of mourning. Gerz is neither a polite nor a reassuring artist. His monument does not engage in the purring of commemorative memory: "I think about it and then I forget." The Invisible Monument is brutal. It stands under the feet of the citizens, every day, from morning till night, at the heart of a city: "This is Germany's foundation." That's what makes it unbearable, what brought a Saar representative to oppose Gerz's project on the grounds that by being invisible, people ran the risk of urinating Saturday's night beer on top of the monument! To which the artist responded: "After all, that's life." However it may be, Gerz's work does not seek to perpetuate eternal guiltiness; it always presents an issue, always on the side of life—life not mortified by oblivion or cowardice but wedded to truth. Here again, the engraved cobblestones, overturned, facing the ground, are the "mime" of the cemeteries that give them their names, and the "mimic" of absence, of everybody's oblivion, of the obliteration, and of the face of the earth and of memory. The Invisible Monument is the shouting "image itself" of its object.

This artist who doesn't make art, today actually accomplishes, with cobblestones and names, almost exactly and in all its potentiality, the Work of Painting according to Alberti: "[Painting] has in itself a thoroughly divine force that not only permits it to actually render, as it is said of friendship, of those who are absent, but also to show, after many centuries, the dead to the living."[16] Each name is an engraved characteristic, and all together they compose the figure—a portrait of absence, faithfully line by line, (in ancient times it was written as *pourtraict*). A simple difference of perspective: Gerz is a painter of memory, he engraves the mind.

8

The monument, its sole "visibility" confined to street plates indicating "Square of the Invisible Monument," is totally precarious. If a hand in the dead of the night unscrews the plates, the monument will seem to vanish, left eventually for an archeologist of the future. Yet this fragility is part of memory itself, after all oblivion is nothing but an effaced inscription. Except that, in this case, the hand removing the plates won't be effacing the impression of a souvenir, but one of oblivion, which silently and invisibly Gerz' monument renders in the present—almost tangible. The attempt to forget the forgotten, that is a whole other thing than remembering.

Here, the spectators of The Invisible Monument—simple

unconcerned passers-by, unconscious, lost to everything and to the work itself, are designated here, again, in truth, as the work itself.

Claude Lanzmann thinks to be a witness is an act. Within a strong tradition of treating the viewer as the innocent recipient of a passive solicitation, Gerz puts forward the act of being a witness. To bestow upon the fact of looking its entire active might. To look: an action for whom the perverse voyeur is not the only one accountable. A person in charge of his gaze.

9

To join together the sundry drawn threads to make an extra loop. Obviously Gerz's art stands at the opposite of consolation. It occupies a place that runs counter to all Freudian conceptions of cathartic beauty, or even Lacanian, regarding the soothing virtue of the art object worth seeing. Rather than "you want to see why yes then see that," where Lacan hooks up the function *trompe-la-faim* or *poire-pour-la-soif of art*, Gerz's art would be "you don't want to see, why yes look at that." An art that doesn't thus make art, which arises on the contrary, as a refusal of being, as art, an justification, to offer through effects of power, beauty or whatever you would want, an excuse or a screen. Society asks for sublimity, insisting that the artist produce—in material monuments intended for public spaces—something in the guise of a mythologizing of itself and its past, often bending the artist to become the surrogate of lost tales.

Art which is not an art of Gerz breaks with all this. Instead of grooming and healing, these monuments undress gaping wounds. Rather than constructing imposing objects, that they impose silence and call for communion, he creates art works that prompt talking and divide. Instead of simply recalling something to someone, these monuments remind someone to something, the witness, the passer-by to his/her duty. Worse, it's the viewer, the passer-by whom they call—to memory. Etc.

Works that recall absence. That flaunt absence.

If these works aim well, invisibility is inevitable. The image is always affirmative. Here lies Gerz's trouble: how does one show what is not, vanishing itself, or oblivious itself, or refusal to see—absence? To expose negation, how? Choose, for instance, to show those who are not here anymore: somehow the image always entails an assertion as to presence. The denial dimension of the image is after all what Alberti roused in behalf of the "memorial" function of painting—it allows to preserve in presence what is dead. In this, every image is a refusal of death and loss—a denial of absence.

To which, with his invisible monuments, Gerz retorts: absence is a real. He says "I have confidence in the idea of loss."[17] You may then undoubtedly assume, and with a certain emphasis, that Gerz "has called into question the traditional language of monuments."[18] Yet, he only puts into question what, by metaphor, one may call his "language:" to question his language, he first had to question the object itself, the monument—it's raison d'être. The rest follows from there.

Thus I could say that these monuments, each in its own way, assert oblivion and loss. Their object is the assertion of a lack-of-object. It then becomes plain that to argue for "absolute resemblance" entails a rather lame, if not entirely untrue, way of speaking, a sticky approach of the imaginary so far. Actually these works "do not resemble to," they do not look "like" they "do not echo any specific voice"—they are the very thing, the thing itself.

Gerz's monuments stand up to an essential trend in contemporary art, namely that which constrains the pondering of modernity from the viewpoint of a resemblance beyond the image, a resemblance that offers as much as a mirror, an absolute similitude with the object, without an identity equation, a resemblance without using "as" and "same," outside of any analogy, likeness or transposition.

I am of the opinion that art aims for the real. On this axis, you may envision imitation as a way for art to aim at the real. By way of the image: that the image functions as well as a screen to the real does not entirely invalidate resemblance as the conductive agency leading to the real. Therefore here we may ask: can art aim at the real, "resemble" the real, that is, resemble the real without imitating it, without neither ostracizing nor uncovering it, thus without an image? The question becomes how to leave resemblance out of the specular? A non-specular resemblance. Something you may dub as arch-resemblance or meta-mimesis.

In short: an art of genuine anti-transposition. These are works that do not show nor say anything: that aim to manifest themselves upon the goal.

A different, nicer persuasion of anti-trans-position—unamendable to metaphor—can be advanced by exposing it as devoid of poetry, and even utterly non-poetical: all in all it is resolutely anti-poetical art.

However, Gerz behaves tactfully vis- à-vis poets and defines his work as "another thing". As for myself, his work, which restlessly enters the tragic heart of the century, finds a ubiquitous place at the very center of today's art.

To conclude, I'll bring forward a dimension peculiar to these works, to them being "monuments" (not at all "anti-monuments"). The actual monuments delight in provocation, as they cast oblivion at the eyes, the reminder of a bygone event, defined, delimited in time. They are not there solely to unceasingly state "do not forget what happened:" because the "fact" is—"it did happen"—these works are obviously useful for its actual construction. By way of the effects they bring about, while disturbing memory silences, they assist in furthering, now, the true dimension. Thus, I would go as far as to say that Gerz's works started up in league not with an historical fact, but with the truth. Instead of assuming that in time the fact of the concentration camps falls from one, sinks into the past, one has to realize that over time the "fact" has intensified, becomes more present every day, more weighty;[19] not because of the constant threat of a comeback, but in that we have to wait for the "fact" to emerge in its full unbearable significance. Art plays its part in this process—*Guernica* has played and still plays its own part as to and, you may say, "in" the Spanish Civil War; just as *Shoah,* I think, is not a documentary "about" horror, as film it belongs to Shoah. There they are, "monuments" that, in a way, constitute what they "monumentalize." Art indeed plays its part: the role of rendering an aspect of truth in the present. To make an object out of a fact—yet precisely: this "fact," this "object" contributes to its being established. Is it the point of view that creates the object? Saussure says that somewhere.

10

The selected works of Gerz carry to the utmost a disjunction between to-give-one-to-see and to-make-one-see: they thus make us see that they themselves give nothing for the tooth of the eye to chew. Irrespective of their extreme radicality they may comply with Klee's classic standards: "Art does not reproduce the visible, it makes the visible."

When presented with works that bring uncertainty to determining whether they are art or trash, you may find a clue in the frugal, yet solid, statement that what "makes you see" is art. Now I will suavely recall that philosophical concepts, as pointed out by Deleuze, also make you see, and consequently, all that makes you see is not art. Precisely, we may argue for an artistic function of the concept (which after all is just tit for tat). If this is so, it would convey a true, serious and consistent weight to the categorization of Gerz's work as "conceptual art." To make visible without recurring to what is visible.

Yet to make us see exactly what? Likewise, Antoni Tapies' remark on abstraction could suit this art positioned at the antipodes of representation: "Even when certain people considered us the farthest from genuine reality, we were in fact the nearest." (*La pratique de l'art*, 1974) To make us see without representing.

Hence the idea of an art outside visibility that makes "genuine reality" visible, a heart of what is visible. Two functions, to make us see and to aim at the real, which fusion: a kind of art that makes us see the real.

What's new and interesting in all this? After all, it may be but a modern variation on the Hegelian theme of art that makes see. Except that, for Hegel, what art makes visible is visibility itself, our reality. And what we are dealing with in here is that the real made visible is something which is not visible, such as absence. Hence we will update art's ambition from the time of the Renaissance and Alberti, namely to represent "that which cannot be seen." Only this "invisibility" art translates into visibility qualifies the sublime and metaphysics—the wind, the tempest or the human soul—whereas the "invisibility" sought by Gerz runs counter to all that, no trace of metaphysics or the sublime in there.

These are works leading to the crux of an art which makes us see neither what is visible nor what is invisible. To spell out the dilemma you could resort to the trite notion of the modernist project which argues: art that makes us see shrugs off visible reality and instead "conveys" ideas and abstractions. Whoever affects absence as an "idea" or an "abstraction" has surely never been in the position of an infant crying after a departed mother, a estranged lover, a mournful griever, in essence, nothing of a human being. Is there anything tougher, more painfully real than absence?

Absence, the work-of-the-art.

## 11

Art that aims at the real and thereby at truth, whether to make us see the real, or to show the truth: this is what Gerz's work achieves and makes achieve. At the same time it makes clear, without words, that maybe it is art's specific task. Everybody knows that there is no reason for truth to be funny and the real pretty as a heart, yet as it is written on one of my T-shirts, "Art is a dirty job, but somebody's got to do it." In brief, an ethics of art.

1. Invisibility, related here to the column vanishing underground, brings about, for all monuments, a thoughtful-provoking consequence: residents will have to explain to visiting friends and to their children; they will have "to unfold a narrative" of the Memorial, a description, telling the story of its disappearance. All things considered, to the monument's visible disappearance from memory follows the bystanders' imperceptible transformation into the memory of the Memorial itself.
2. After long and difficult research both in the archives and in the field, the exact number of Jewish graveyards was ascertained by Jochen Gerz with the aid of an active group of students from The Fine Arts Academy of Saarbrücken. Let's mention as a passing remark that the German State was unable to provide accurate information. Besides, an additional paradox, the work of an artist did more than circumvent the hampering of bureaucratic deficiencies: it compelled the German government to acknowledge the number 2146, to put it on its records, to make it official.
3. There is only one book listing the 2146 Jewish cemeteries existing in Germany prior to 1939: Gerz, Jochen, *2146 Steine, Mahnmal gegen Rassismus, Saarbrücken*, Sttutgart: Gerd Hatje, 1993.
4. This may seem obvious for the first two works, but in the case of The Living Monument of Biron, the monument to the dead is absolutely identical to the old one, and therefore there is nothing to see. Only the red enamelled plates attract attention, and then only for reading them. I even suspect that Gerz is more concerned with the firmness of the screws holding the plates to the stone than with their color arrangement (maybe they are red because it was cheaper).
5. Gerz, Jochen, *La Question secrète, Le Monument vivant de Biron*, Paris: Actes Sud, 1996, p. 149.
6. Michaud, Yves, "L'art auquel on ne fait pas attention," in *Critique* 416, 01/1982.
7. Gerz himself, back in 1972, produced a significant work on the subject: *The Dachau Project*. Lanzmann, with film, however, opened the debate to a vast audience.
8. It would have seem that only Godard could have revealed the reality entrenched in the heart of cinema by highlighting the extreme paradox of a film industry which delivered no image of this century's central event, namely the concentration camps.
9. Besides work such as that of Boltanski or the accumulations of Arman, started after WW II, we are dealing here with a dimension that insists that the artist's oeuvre be removed from such concerns, or with exhibitions like the one organized by Jean Clair, *Identité et altérité, les images du corps:1895-1995*, at the Venice Biennial in 1995.

10. Representation, or the return to representation, seems haunted by this dimension; certainly such portraits are still painted if one looks for them; Bacon delves beyond specularity, beyond resemblance, into something akin to a formless truth of the flesh. As for Baselitz, his huge family portraits are painted and presented topsy-turvy, head down. While this "question" should not turn into a universal elucidative key, it none the less sets the standard of a dichotomy: there is an aesthetic open to the issue of the concentration camps, and then there is an other one that precludes the subject. Needless to say that I'm not much inclined to consider the "other" aesthetic as being relevant to art.
11. Gerz, J., *La Question secrète*, p. 157. As for "resemblance," I'll bring to notice another issue posited by The Anti-Fascist Memorial: its sinking, deliberated and unhurried, movement running counter to the upstanding verticalness usually mandatory in such cases. This particular so startled some city representatives that they decided to cast a friendly vote on the project only if the artist instead of diving down the column, acquiesced to its ascending above ground "like a flower."
12. Gerz, J., *La Question secrète*. In there all the answers are listed.
13. Gerz conceived the work as one in progress: each new villager would answer "the secret question," the response being engraved on a plate and affixed on the monument. It's ironic that Biron, a French village active in the Résistance, owes its War Memorial to a German artist. A good omen.
14. For a general understanding of the monument, see my interview (and Jacqueline Lichtenstein's) with Jochen Gerz: "La place du monument invisible" in *Art Press International* 179, Paris, 1993, p. 10-46.
15. The controversy on The Berlin Holocaust Memorial dedicated to the victims of Nazism (to all "victims," including those German soldiers who died in action) and commissioned by the German government (it depicts a woman grieving her dead child) gives ample evidence of the danger.
16. Alberti, Leon Battista, *Della Pintura*, book II: 25, Paris: Macula, 1994.
17. Gerz, J., La Question secrète, p. 167.
18. Schulz, Bernhard, "Des remémorisations du passé" in *Opus International* 129, 1992.
19. The Nuremberg Trials (1945-1949) actually did not reveal the full extent of "The Final Solution." Only in the 70s its true nature began to emerge.

# *Il n'y a pas de rapport religieux*

SLAVOJ ZIZEK

Since, as Lacan claims in his Seminar XX: *Encore*, Woman is one of the names of God, would it not be logical to conclude that, in the same way that there is no sexual rapport, there is also no religious rapport? Perhaps, the uncanny fact of Christ's Crucifixion stands for the silent admission of this fact. In order fully to appreciate the uniqueness of the figure of Christ, let us start with Gilles Deleuze's exemplary analysis of Chaplin's late films:

> Between the small Jewish barber and the dictator in *The Great Dictator*, the difference is as negligeable as that between their respective moustaches. Yet it results in two situations as infinitely remote, as far opposed as those of victim and executioner. Likewise, in *Monsieur Verdoux*, the difference between the two aspects or demeanors of the same man, the lady-assassin and the loving husband of a paralyzed wife, is so thin that all his wife's intuition is required for the premonition that somehow he "changed." /.../ the burning question of *Limelight* is: what is that "nothing," that sign of age, that small difference of triteness, on account of which the funny clown's number changes into a tedious spectacle?[1]

## *Il n'y a pas de rapport religieux*

The paradigmatic case of this imperceptible "almost nothing" are the old paranoiac science-fiction films from the early 50s about aliens occupying a small American town: they look and act like normal Americans, we can distinguish them only via the reference to some minor detail. It is Ernst Lubitsch's *To Be Or Not To Be* which brings this logic to its dialectical climax. In one of the funniest scenes of the film, the pretentious Polish actor who, as the part of a secret mission, has to impersonate the cruel high Gestapo officer Erhardt, does this impersonation in an exaggerated way,

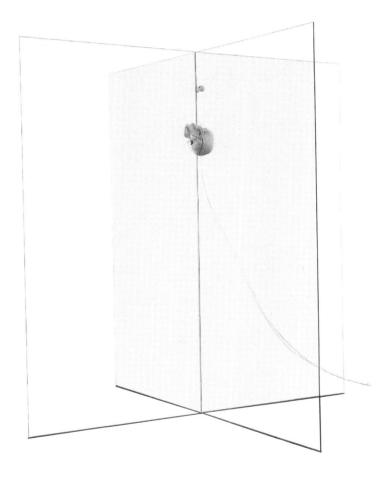

DAMIEN HIRST, *Skullduggery*, glass cross, skull, ping-pong balls, compressor, 2000

reacting to the remarks of his interlocutor about his cruel treatment of the Poles with loud vulgar laughter and a satisfied contestation, "So they call me Concentration Camp Erhardt, ha-ha!" We, the spectators, take this for a ridiculous caricature—however, when, later in the film the REAL Erhardt appears, he reacts to his interlocutors in exactly the same way. Although the "real" Erhardt in a way imitates his imitation, "plays himself." This uncanny coincidence makes all the more palpable the absolute gap that separates him from the poor Polish impersonator. In Hitchcock's *Vertigo*, we find a more tragic version of the same uncanny coincidence: the low-class Judy who, under the pressure exerted from and out of her love for Scottie, endeavors to look and act like the high-class fatal and ethereal Madeleine, turns out to BE Madeleine: they are the same person, since the "true" Madeleine Scottie encountered was already a fake. However, this identity of Judy and Judy-Madeleine, this difference between the two fakes, again renders all the more palpable the absolute otherness of Madeleine with regard to Judy—the Madeleine that is given nowhere, that is present just in the guise of the ethereal "aura" that envelops Judy-Madeleine. The Real is the appearance as appearance, it not only appears WITHIN appearances, but it is also NOTHING BUT its own appearance—it is just a certain GRIMACE of reality, a certain imperceptible, unfathomable, ultimately illusory feature that accounts for the absolute difference within the identity. So, with regard to the grimace of real/reality, it is crucial to keep open the reversibility of this formulation. In a first approach, reality is a grimace of the real—the real, structured/distorted into the "grimace" we call reality through the pacifying symbolic network, somehow like the Kantian *Ding-an-sich* structured into what we experience as objective reality through the transcendental network. In a second, deeper approach, things appear exactly the same as in a first approach—with, however, a little twist: the real itself is nothing but a grimace of reality, i.e., the obstacle, the "bone in the throat" which forever distorts our perception of reality, introducing anamorphic stains in it, or the pure

Schine of Nothing that only "shines through" reality, since it is "in itself" thoroughly without substance.

A homologous inversion is to be accomplished apropos of the "illusion of the real," of the postmodern denouncing every (effect of) the Real as an illusion: what Lacan opposes to it is the much more subversive notion of the Real of the illusion itself.[2] Consider the fashionable argument according to which Real Socialism failed because it endeavored to impose onto reality an illusory utopian vision of humanity, not taking into account the way real people are structured through the force of tradition: on the contrary, Real Socialism failed because it was—in its Stalinist version—ALL TOO REALISTIC because it underestimated the REAL of the "illusions" which continued to determine human activity ("bourgeois individualism," etc.), and conceived of the "construction of socialism" as a ruthlessly "realistic" mobilization and exploitation of the individuals in order to build a new order. One is thus tempted to claim that, while Lenin still remained faithful to the "real of the (Communist) illusion," to its emancipatory utopian potential, Stalin was a simple "realist," engaged in a ruthless power-struggle.

Each of the two parts of Freud's inaugural dream on Irma's injection concludes with a figuration of the Real. In the conclusion of the first part, this is obvious: the look into Irma's throat renders the Real in the guise of the primordial flesh, the palpitation of the life substance as the Thing itself, in its disgusting dimension of a cancerous outgrowth. However, in the second part, the comic symbolic exchange/interplay of the three doctors also ends up with the Real, this time in its opposite aspect—the Real of writing, of the meaningless formula of trimethylamine. The difference hinges on the different starting point: if we end with the Imaginary (the mirror-confrontation of Freud and Irma), we get the Real in its imaginary dimension, as a horrifying primordial image that cancels the imagery itself; if we start with the Symbolic (the exchange of arguments between the three doctors), we get the signifier itself transformed into the Real of a meaningless letter/formula. Needless to add that these two figures are the very two opposite aspects of the Lacanian Real: the abyss of the primordial Life-Thing and the meaningless letter/formula (as in the Real of modern science). And, perhaps, one should add to them the third Real, the "Real of the illusion," the Real of a pure semblance, of a spectral dimension which shines through our common reality. There are thus THREE modalities of the Real, i.e., the triad IRS reflects itself within the order of the Real, so that we have the "real Real" (the horrifying Thing, the primordial object, like Irma's throat), the "symbolic Real" (the signifier reduced to a senseless formula, like the quantum physics formulas which can no longer be translated back into—or related to—the everyday experience of our life-world), AND the "imaginary Real" (the mysterious *je ne sais quoi*, the unfathomable "something" that introduces a self-division into an ordinary object, so that the sublime dimension shines through it). If, then, as Lacan put it, Gods are of the Real, the Christian Trinity also has to be read through the lenses of this Trinity of the Real: God the Father is the "real Real" of the violent primordial Thing; God the Son is the "imaginary Real" of the pure Schein, the "almost nothing" through which the sublime shines through his miserable body; the Holy Ghost is the "symbolic Real" of the community of believers.

A homologous reversal is also to be accomplished if we are to conceive properly the paradoxical status of the Real as impossible. The deconstructionist ethical edifice is based on the IMPOSSIBILITY of the act: the act never happens, it is impossible for it to occur, it is always deferred, about to come, there is forever the gap that separates the impossible fullness of the Act from the limited dimension of our contingent pragmatic intervention (say, the unconditional ethical demand of the Other from the pragmatic political intervention with which we answer it). The fantasy of metaphysics is precisely that the impossible Act CAN or COULD happen, that it would have happened if it were not for some contingent empirical obstacle; the task of the deconstructionist analysis is then to demonstrate how what appears (and is misperceived) as a contingent empirical obstacle actually gives body to a proto-transcendental a priori—such apparently contingent obstacles HAVE to occur, the impossibility is structural, not empirical-contingent. Say, the illusion of anti-Semitism is that social antagonisms are introduced by the Jewish intervention, so that, if we eliminate Jews, the fully realized non-antagonistic harmonious social body will take place; against this misperception, the critical analysis should demonstrate how the anti-Semitic figure of the Jew just gives body to the structural impossibility constitutive of the social order.

It seems that Lacan also fits perfectly this logic: does the illusory fullness of the imaginary fantasy not cover up a structural gap, and does psychoanalysis not assert the heroic acceptance of the fundamental gap and/or structural impossibility as the very condition of desire? Is this, exactly, not the "ethics of the Real"—the ethics of accepting the Real of a structural impossibility? However, what Lacan ultimately aims at is precisely the opposite; let's take the case of love. Lovers usually dream that in some mythical Otherness ("another time, another place"), their love would have found its true fulfillment, that it is only the present contingent circumstances which prevent this fulfillment; and is the Lacanian lesson here not that one should accept this obstacle as structurally necessary, that there is NO "other place" of fulfillment, that this Otherness is the very Otherness of the fantasy? No: the "Real as impossible" means here that THE IMPOSSIBLE DOES HAPPEN, that "miracles" like Love (or political revolution: "in some respects, a revolution is a miracle," Lenin said in 1921) DO occur. From "impossible TO happen" we thus pass to "the impossible HAPPENS"—this, and not the structural obstacle forever deferring the final resolution, is the most difficult thing to accept: "We'd forgotten how to be in readiness even for miracles to happen."[3]

The act proper is thus to be opposed to other modalities of the act: the hysterical acting out, the psychotic *passage à l'acte*, the symbolic act. In the hysterical acting out, the subject stages, in a kind of theatrical performance, the compromise solution of the trauma she is unable to cope with. In the psychotic *passage à l'acte*, the deadlock is so debilitating that the subject cannot even imagine a way out—the only thing he can do is to strike blindly in the real, to release his frustration in the meaningless outburst of destructive energy. The symbolic act is best conceived of as the purely formal, self-referential, gesture of the self-assertion of one's subjective position. Let us take a situation of the political defeat of some working class initiative; what one should accomplish at this moment to reassert one's identity is precisely the symbolic act: stage a common event in which some shared ritual (song or whatsoever) is performed, an event which contains no positive political program—its message is only the purely performative assertion: "We are still here, faithful to our mission, the space is still open for our activity to come!" Mark Herman's *Brassed Off* focuses on the relationship between the "real" political struggle (the miners' struggle against the threatening pit closure legitimized in the terms of technological progress) and the idealized symbolic expression of the miners' community, their playing the brass band. At first, the two aspects seem to be opposed: to the miners caught in the struggle for their economic survival, the "Only music matters!" attitude of their old band leader dying of lung cancer appears as a vain fetishized insistence of the empty symbolic form deprived of its social substance. However, once miners lose their political struggle, the "music matters" attitude, their insistence to go on playing and participating in the national competition, turns into a defying symbolic gesture, a proper act of asserting fidelity to their political struggle—as one of the miners puts it, when there is no hope, there are just principles to follow…In short, the symbolic act occurs when we arrive at this crisscross, or, rather, short-circuit of the two levels, so that insistence on the empty form itself (we'll continue playing our brass band, whatever happens…) becomes the sign of fidelity to the content (to the struggle against the closures, for the continuation of the miners' way of life). In contrast to all these three modes, the act proper is the only one which restructures the very symbolic coordinates of the agent's situation: it is an intervention in the course of which the agent's identity itself is radically changed.

And it's exactly the same with belief: the lesson of Graham Greene's novels is that religious belief, far from being the pacifying consolation, is the most traumatic thing to accept. Therein resides the ultimate failure of Neil Jordan's *The End of an Affair*, which accomplishes two changes with regard to Greene's novel upon which it is based: it displaces the ugly birthmark (and its miraculous disappearance after a kiss by Sarah) from the atheist preacher to the private investigator's son, plus it condenses two persons (the atheist preacher whom Sarah visited after her shocking encounter with the miracle, i.e., the success of her wager after she finds her lover dead, and the older Catholic priest who tries to console Maurice, the narrator, and Sarah's husband after her death) into one, the preacher whom Sarah is secretly visiting and who is mistaken by Maurice for her lover. This replacement of the agnostic preacher by a priest thoroughly misses the point of Sarah's visits: in a dialectic of faith that is Greene's trademark, she starts to visit him precisely because of his ferocious anti-theism: she wants desperately to ESCAPE her faith, the miraculous proof of God's existence, so she takes refuge with the avowed atheist—with the predictable result that not only does he fail in delivering her of her faith, but that, at the novel's end, he himself becomes a believer (THIS is also the reason why the miracle of the disappearing birthmark has to take place on HIS face!). The psychoanalytic name for such a "miracle," for an intrusion which momentarily suspends the causal network of our daily lives, is, of course, trauma. In his *Zollikoner Seminare*, edited by Medard Boss, Heidegger dismisses Freud as a causal determinist:

> He postulates for the conscious human phenomena that they can be explained without gaps, i.e., the continuity of causal connections. Since there are no such connections "in the consciousness," he has to invent "the unconscious," in which there have to be the causal links without gaps.[4]

Here, of course, Heidegger completely misses the way the Freudian "unconscious" is grounded in the traumatic encounter of an Otherness whose intrusion precisely breaks, interrupts, the continuity of the causal link: what we get in the "unconscious" is not a complete, uninterrupted, causal link, but the repercussions, the after-shocks, of traumatic interruptions.[5] Although there is a similarity between this Lacanian Real and the notion of the "priority of the objective" elaborated by Adorno, Heidegger's most embittered critic, it is this very similarity that renders all the more palpable the gap that separates them. Adorno's basic endeavor is to reconcile the materialist "priority of the objective" with the idealist legacy of the subjective "mediation" of all objective reality: everything we experience as directly-immediately given is already mediated, posited through a network of differences; every theory that asserts our access to immediate reality, be it the phenomenological Wesensschau or the empiricist perception of elementary sensual data, is false. On the other hand, Adorno also rejects the idealist notion that all objective content is posited/produced by the subject—such a stance also fetishizes subjectivity itself into a given immediacy. This is the reason why Adorno opposes the Kantian a priori of the transcendental categories which mediate our access to reality (and thus constitute what we experience as reality): for Adorno, the Kantian transcendental a priori does not simply absolutize the subjective mediation—it obliterates its own historical mediation. The table of Kantian transcendental categories is not a pre-historical "pure" a priori, but a historically "mediated" conceptual network, i.e., a network embedded in and engendered by a determinate historical constellation. How, then, are we to think TOGETHER the radical mediation of all objectivity and the materialist "priority of the objective"? The solution is that this "priority" is the very result of mediation brought to its end, the kernel of resistance that we cannot experience directly, but only in the guise of the absent point of reference on account of which every mediation ultimately FAILS.

# *Il n'y a pas de rapport religieux*

It is a standard argument against Adorno's "negative dialectics" to reproach it for its inherent inconsistency; Adorno's answer to it is quite appropriate: stated as a definitive doctrine, as a result, "negative dialectics" effectively IS "inconsistent"—the way to properly grasp it is to conceive of it as the description of a process of thought (in Lacanese, to include the position of enunciation involved in it). "Negative dialectics" designates a position which includes its own failure, i.e., which produces the truth-effect through its very failure. To put it succinctly: one tries to grasp/conceive the object of thought; one fails, missing it, and through these very failures the place of the targeted object is encircled, its contours become discernible. So what one is tempted to do here is to introduce the Lacanian notion of the "barred" subject ($S$) and the object as real/impossible: the Adornian distinction between immediately accessible "positive" objectivity and the objectivity targeted in the "priority of the objective" is the very Lacanian distinction between (symbolically mediated) reality and the impossible Real. Furthermore, does the Adornian notion that the subject retains its subjectivity only insofar as it is "incompletely" subject, insofar as some kernel of objectivity resists its grasp, not point towards the subject as constitutively "barred"?

There are two ways out of the deadlock in which Adorno's "negative dialectics" ends, the Habermasian one and the Lacanian one. Habermas, who well perceived Adorno's inconsistency, his self-destructive critique of Reason which cannot account for itself, proposed as a solution the pragmatic a priori of the communicative normativity, a kind of Kantian regulative ideal presupposed in every intersubjective exchange. Lacan, on the contrary, elaborates the concept of what Adorno deployed as dialectical paradoxes: the concept of the "barred" subject who exists only through its own impossibility; the concept of the Real as the inherent, not external, limitation of reality.

At the level of theology, this shift from external to inherent limitation is accomplished by Christianity. In Judaism, God remains the transcendent irrepresentable Other, i.e., as Hegel was right to emphasize, Judaism is the religion of the Sublime: it tries to render the suprasensible dimension not through the overwhelming excess of the sensible, like the Indian statues with dozens of hands, etc., but in a purely negative way, by renouncing the images altogether. Christianity, however, renounces this God of Beyond, this Real behind the curtain of the phenomena; it acknowledges that there is NOTHING beyond the appearance—nothing BUT the imperceptible X that changes Christ, this ordinary man, into God. In the ABSOLUTE identity of man and God, the divine is the pure Schein of another dimension that shines through Christ, this miserable creature. It is only here that the iconoclasm is truly brought to its conclusion: what is effectively "beyond the image" is that X that makes the man Christ God. In this precise sense, Christianity inverses the Jewish sublimation into a radical desublimation: not desublimation in the sense of the simple reduction of God to man, but desublimation in the sense of the descendence of the sublime Be-

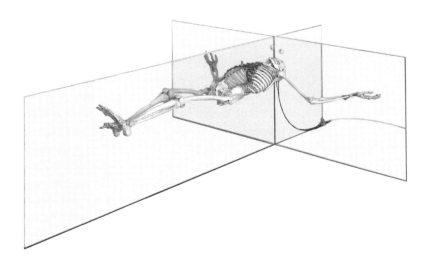

DAMIEN HIRST, *Death is Irrelevant*, skeleton, glass cross, ping-pong balls, compressor, 2000

yond to the everyday level. Christ is a "ready made God" (as Boris Groys put it), he is fully human, inherently indistinguishable from other humans in exactly the same way Judy is indistinguishable from Madeleine in *Vertigo*, or the "true" Erhardt is indistinguishable from his impersonator in *To Be Or Not to Be*—it is only the imperceptible "something," a pure appearance which cannot ever be grounded in a substantial property, that makes him divine. THIS is why Christianity is the religion of love and of comedy: as examples from Lubitsch and Chaplin demonstrate, there is always something comic in this unfathomable difference that undermines the established identity (Judy IS Madeleine, Hynkel IS the Jewish barber). And love is to be opposed here to desire: desire is always caught in the logic of "this is not that," it thrives in the gap that forever separates the obtained satisfaction from the sought-for satisfaction, while love FULLY ACCEPTS that "this IS that"—that the woman with all her weaknesses and common features IS the Thing I unconditionally love; that Christ, this miserable man, IS the living God. Again, to avoid a fatal misunderstanding: the point is not that we should "renounce transcendence" and fully accept the limited human person as our love object, since "this is all there is": transcendence is not abolished, but rendered ACCESSIBLE[6]—it shines through in this very clumsy and miserable being that I love.

Christ is thus not "man PLUS God": what becomes visible in him is simply the divine dimension in man "as such." So, far from being the Highest in man, the purely spiritual dimension towards which all man strive, the "divinity" is rather a kind of obstacle, of a "bone in the throat"—it is something, that unfathomable X, on account of which man cannot ever fully become MAN, self-identical. The point is not that, due to the limitation of his mortal sinful nature, man cannot ever become fully divine, but that, due to the divine spark in him, man cannot ever fully become MAN. Christ as man = God is the unique case of full humanity (*ecce homo,* as Pontius Pilatus put it to the mob demanding the lynching of Christ). For that reason, after his death, there is no place for any

God of Beyond: all that remains is the Holy Spirit, the community of believers onto which the unfathomable aura of Christ passes once it is deprived of its bodily incarnation (or, to put it in the Freudian terms, once it can no longer rely on the *Anlehnung* onto Christ's body, in the same sense as, for Freud, the drive which aims at the unconditional satisfaction, always has to "lean on" a particular, contingent material object which acts as the source of its satisfaction).

This reading has radical consequences for the notion of afterlife. The often noted enigmatic lapse in Judaism concerns afterlife: its sacred texts NEVER mention afterlife—we have a religion which seems to renounce the very basic feature of what religion is supposed to do, i.e., bring us consolation by promising us a happy afterlife. And it is crucial to reject as secondary falsification any notion that Christianity DOES return to the tradition of afterlife (individuals will be judged by God, and then enter either Hell or Paradise). As it was already noted by, among others, Kant, such a notion of Christianity which involves the just payment for our deeds, reduces it to just another religion of the moral accountancy, of the just reward or punishment for our deeds. If one conceives of the Holy Spirit radically enough, there is simply NO PLACE in the Christian edifice for afterlife.

In other words, tragedy and comedy are also to be opposed along the axis of the opposition between desire and drive. As Lacan emphasized all along his teaching, not only is desire inherently "tragic" (condemned to its ultimate failure), tragedy itself (in all the classic cases, from Oedipus and Antigone through Hamlet up to Claudel's *Coufontaine*-trilogy) is ultimately always the tragedy of desire. Drive, on the contrary, is inherently COMIC in its "closing the loop" and suspending the gap of desire, in its assertion of the coincidence, identity even, between the sublime and the everyday object. Of course, the gap persists in drive, in the guise of the distance between its aim—satisfaction—and its goal—the object on which it "leans" (it is because of this gap that drive is forever condemned to the circular movement); however, this gap, instead of opening up the infinite metonymy of desire, sustains the closed loop (or warp) of the drive. In Kafka's "A Fasting Showman", towards the end of the endless process of fasting, the dying showman reveals his secret:

> '...I have to fast, I can't do anything else,' said the fasting showman. 'What a fellow you are,' said the overseer, 'and why can't you do anything else?' 'Because,' said the fasting showman, lifting his head a little and speaking with his lips pursed, as if for a kiss, right into the overseer's ear, so that no syllable might be lost, 'because I couldn't find any food I liked. If I had found any, believe me, I should have made no bones about it and stuffed myself like you or anyone else.' These were his last words...[7]

What strikes the eye here is the contrast with Kafka's most famous text, "Before the Law" from The Trial, in which, towards the end of the lifelong waiting in front of the Door of the Law, the gatekeeper also whispers into the ears of the dying man from the country the secret of the Door (they were made only for him, no one else could have been admitted there, so after his death, they will be closed): in "A Fasting Showman," it is the dying man himself who reveals his secret to his keeper-overseer, while in The Trial, it is the keeper-overseer who reveals the secret to the dying man. Where does this opposition come from, if, in both cases, the secret revealed at the end concerns a certain Void (the lack of the proper food, there is nothing beyond the door)? The fasting showman stands for drive at its purest: he gives body to the Lacanian distinction between "not eating" and "eating the Nothing", i.e., by fasting, by rejecting every offered object-food because *ce n'est pas ça*, he eats Nothing itself, the void which sets in motion desire—he repeatedly circulates around the central void. The man from the country, on the contrary, is a hysteric whose desire is obsessed by the Secret (the Thing) Beyond the Door. So, contrary to the misleading first impression, Kafka's fasting showman is NOT an anorexic: anorexia is one of today's forms of hysteria (the classic Freudian hysteria reacts on the traditional figure of the patriarchal master, while anorexia reacts to the reign of the expert-knowledge).

The key distinction to be maintained here can be exemplified by the (apparent) opposite of religion, the intense sexual experience. Eroticization relies on the inversion-into-self of the movement directed at an external goal: the movement itself becomes its own goal. (When, instead of simply gently shaking the hand offered to me by the beloved person, I hold to it and repeatedly squeeze it, my activity will be automatically experienced as—welcome or, perhaps, intrusively unwelcome—eroticization: what I do is change the goal-oriented activity into an end-in-itself.) Therein resides the difference between the goal and the aim of a drive: say, with regard to the oral drive, its goal may be to eliminate hunger, but its aim is the satisfaction provided by the activity of eating (sucking, swallowing) itself. One can imagine the two satisfactions entirely separated: when, in a hospital, I am fed intravenously, my hunger is satisfied, but not my oral drive; when, on the contrary, a small child rhythmically sucks the comforter, the only satisfaction he gets is that of the drive. This gap that separates aim from goal "eternalizes" drive, transforming the simple instinctual movement which finds peace and calm when it reaches its goal (say, the full stomach) into the process which gets caught in its own loop and insists on endlessly repeating itself. The crucial feature to take note of here is that this inversion cannot be formulated in the terms of the primordial lack and the series of metonymic objects trying (and, ultimately, failing) to fill in its void. When the eroticized body of my partner starts to function as the object around which drive circulates, this does NOT mean that his/her ordinary ("pathological," in the Kantian sense of the term) flesh-and-blood body is "transubstantiated" into a contingent embodiment of the sublime impossible Thing, holding (filling out) its empty place. Let us take a direct "vulgar" example: when a (heterosexual male) lover is fascinated with his partner's vagina, "never getting enough of it,"

*Il n'y a pas de rapport religieux*

prone not only to penetrate it, but to explore it and caress it in all possible ways, the point is NOT that, in a kind of deceptive short-circuit, he mistakes the piece of skin, hair and meat for the Thing itself—his lover's vagina is, in all its bodily materiality, "the thing itself," not the spectral appearing of another dimension; what makes it an "infinitely" desirable object whose "mystery" cannot ever be fully penetrated, is its non-identity to itself, i.e., the way it is never directly "itself." (Of course, it's not the physical appearance of the vagina which matters: what matters is that this vagina belongs to the beloved person. In other words, and to indulge in a rather tasteless mental experiment: if I were to discover that the same looking vagina belongs to a different person (or that the person that I love has a different vagina), then this same vagina would no longer exert the unconditional fascination. What this means is that drive and desire are nonetheless inherently interwoven: not only does desire always rely on some partial drives which provide its "stuff"; drives also function only insofar as they refer to the subject whose desire I desire.) The gap which "eternalizes" drive, turning it into the endlessly repetitive circular movement around the object, is not the gap that separates the void of the Thing from its contingent embodiments, but the gap that separates the very "pathological" object FROM ITSELF, in the same way that, as we have just seen, Christ is not the contingent material ("pathological") embodiment of the suprasensible God: his "divine" dimension is reduced to the aura of a pure Schain.

Therein resides the problem with Bernard Baas's outstanding Kantian reading of Lacan in his *De la Chose à l'objet*,[8] this heroic endeavor to think together the Kantian "transcendental" reading of Lacan with the problematic of the presubjective drive, of that obscure process in the course of which a living body "explodes" into a self-sentient organism which is at the same time inside and outside itself (it is part of its objective environs in which it exists as an object, while, at the same time, it contains the world in its field of vision). We are thus dealing with what Lacan refers to as the mysterious "doubling/*la doublure*"⁹ of the living body: a gap, distance, is introduced, a gap which involves the paradoxical topology of the Moebius band or Klein's bottle.¹⁰ It is in this "doubling" which is not yet the subjective redoubling characteristic of self-reflection and/or self-consciousness, that Lacan discerns the fundamental structure of the "acephalous" drive whose best metaphor are a pair of lips kissing themselves. The mysterious intermediate status of drive resides in the fact that, while we are NOT YET dealing with the subject submitted to the symbolic Law, condemned to the eternal search for the primordial lost object ("Thing") which is already missing in reality, we are also NO LONGER dealing with the immediate self-enclosure of a biological organism: from the standpoint of "mere (biological) life," a certain excess is already at work here, a certain "too much," the addiction to a surplus which can no longer be contained—what is "drive" if not the name for an excessive "pressure" which derails/disturbs the purely biological life-rhythm. Eric Santner connects this excess to the old Heraclitian formula *hen diapheron heauto*, to which Plato refers in his *Symposium*, and which Hoelderlin, in his *Hyperion*, translates as *das Eine in sich Unterschiedene*—the one differentiated in itself.¹¹ And, as Santner points out, when Hoelderlin endorses this formula as the very definition of beauty, the point is not that artists reconcile the opposites and tensions in the aesthetic Totality of a harmonious Whole, but, quite on the contrary, that they construct a place in which people can ecstatically perceive the traumatic excess around which their life turns. Along these lines, Santner proposes a new reading of Hoelderlin's famous lines from his hymn *Andenken*: *Was bleibet aber, stiften die Dichter* / "But poets establish what remains." The standard reading, of course, is that, after the events, poets are able to perceive the situation from the mature standpoint after the fact, i.e., from the safe distance when the historical meaning of the events become clear. What if, however, what remains is the remainder itself, what Schelling called the "indivisible remainder," that which STICKS OUT from the organic Whole, the excess which cannot be incorporated/integrated into the socio-historical Totality, so that, far from providing the harmonious total image of an epoch, poetry gives voice to that which an epoch was UNABLE to include in its narrative(s)? The fact that the original formula (*hen diapheron heauto*) is Heraclitian should make us attentive: one should read it "anachronistically," against the grain, i.e., NOT in its original pre-Socratic sense of the harmony of the All which emerges from the very struggle and tension of its parts, but as focused on that excess which prevents the One from ever turning into a harmonious All. It is as if Heraclitus' words are to be conceived of as a fragment pointing towards the future, coming from the future: only an "anachronistic" reading from the future can discern its true meaning.

How, then, can Baas bring together this notion of drive and his earlier brilliant Kantian reading of Lacan which emphasizes the structural homology between the Freudian-Lacanian Thing and the Kantian noumenal Thing-in-itself: the Thing is nothing but its own lack, the elusive specter of the lost primordial object of desire engendered by the symbolic Law/Prohibition, and *l'objet petit a* is the Lacanian "transcendental scheme" which mediates between the a priori void of the impossible Thing and the empirical objects that give us (dis)pleasure—*objets a* are empirical objects contingently elevated to the dignity of the Thing, so that they start to function as embodiments of the impossible Thing?[12] Baas's solution is predictable: in its self-enclosed circulation, drive achieves its aim by repeatedly missing its goal, which means that it rotates around a central Void, and this Void is the Void of/as the impossible/real Thing, prohibited/lost once the subject emerges through entering the symbolic order...At this point, however, one should insist that the "doubling," the topological torsion which brings about the "excess" of life we call "drive," CANNOT be equated to (or grounded in) the symbolic Law which prohibits the impossible maternal Real Thing: the gap opened up by this "doubling" is NOT the void of the Thing prohibited by the symbolic Law. One is almost tempted to say that the ultimate function of the symbolic Law is to enable us to AVOID the debilitating deadlock of drive—the symbolic Law already reacts to a certain inherent impediment on account of which the animal instinct somehow gets "stuck" and explodes in the excessive repetitive movement, it enables the subject to magically transform this repetitive movement through which the subject is stuck with and for the drive's cause-object, into the eternal open search for the (lost/prohibited) object of desire. To put it in a slightly different way: while Baas is right to insist that the "doubling" of the drive always occurs within the order of the signifier, he equates too quickly signifier with the symbolic order grounded in the Law/Prohibition: what Lacan was endeavoring to elaborate in the last two decades of his teaching was precisely the status of a signifier not yet contained within the symbolic Law/Prohibition. Nowhere is this distinction clearer than apropos of sublimation (if we follow Lacan in defining it as the elevation of an (empirical) object to the dignity of the Thing):[13] the drive does NOT "elevate an (empirical) object into the dignity of the Thing"—it rather chooses as its object an object which has in itself the circular structure of rotating around a void.

We all know the phrase "the devil resides in the details"—implying that, in an agreement, you should be attentive to the proverbial small letter specifications and conditions at the bottom of the page which may contain unpleasant surprises, and, for all practical purposes, nullify what the agreement offers. Does, however, this phrase hold also for theology? Is it really that God is discernible in the overall harmony of the universe, while the Devil sticks in small features which, while insignificant from the global perspective, can mean terrible suffering for us, individuals? With regard to Christianity, at least, one is tempted to turn around this formula: God resides in details—in the overall drabness and indifference of the universe, we discern the divine dimension in barely perceptible details—a kind smile here, an unexpected helpful gesture there...The Turin Shroud with the alleged photographic imprint of Christ is perhaps the ultimate case of this "divine detail," of the "little bit of the real"—the very hot debates about it neatly fall into the triad IRS: the Imaginary (is the image discernible on it the faithful reproduction of Christ?), the Real (when was the material made? Is the test which demonstrated that the linen was woven in the 14th century conclusive?), the Symbolic (the narrative of the Shroud's complicated destiny through the centuries). The true problem, however, resides in the potential catastrophic consequences for the Church itself if the tests will indicate again that the Shroud is authentic (from Christ's time and place): there are traces of "Christ"'s blood on it, and some biochemists are already working on its DNA—so what will this DNA say about Christ's FATHER (not to mention the prospect of CLONING Christ)?

    Does, however, this minimal self-distance of a living being into which this excess inscribes itself, this gap or redoubling of life into "ordinary" life and the spectral "undead" life, not display the structure of what Marx described as the "commodity fetishism"—an ordinary object acquires the aura, another incorporeal dimension starts to shine through it? As Lacan himself emphasized,[14] the answer is that commodity fetishism itself parasitizes upon the structure of "immanent transcendence" which pertains to drive as such: in certain social conditions, the products of human labor mobilize this function, appearing as the universe of commodities. With regard to the figure of Christ, this reference to the universe of commodities also enables us to reactualize Marx's old idea that Christ is like money among men—ordinary commodities: in the same way money as universal equivalent directly embodies/assumes the excess ("Value") that makes an object a commodity, Christ directly embodies/assumes the excess that makes the human animal a proper human being. In both cases, then, the universal equivalent exchanges/gives itself for all other excesses—in the same way money is the commodity "as such," Christ is man "as such"; in the same way that the universal equivalent has to be a commodity deprived of any use value, Christ has taken over the excess of Sin of ALL men precisely insofar as he was the Pure one, without excess, simplicity itself.

In order to elucidate the elementary structure of this excess, let us turn to Jonathan Lear who deploys a powerful critique of the Freudian "death drive": Freud hypostasizes into a positive teleological principle the purely negative fact of breaks and interruptions which cannot be directly contained/integrated in the "normal" teleologically oriented psychic economy; instead of accepting the fact of purely contingent interruptions which undermine the teleological functioning of the human psyche, he fantasizes a higher positive tendency/principle that accounts for these disruptions ("death drive").[15] Lear accuses Lacan of the same reifying positivisation of the gap/break into a positive "Beyond" apropos of the notion of the Thing as the Beyond, the unattainable hard kernel of the Real around which signifiers circulate. Instead of accepting that there is always some rest which cannot be accounted for in the terms of the "principle(s)" governing psychic life, Freud invents a higher principle that should effectively encompass the entire psychic life. In a nicely elaborated parallel between Aristotle and Freud, and borrowing the term from Laplanche, Lear specifies this operation as that of introducing the "enigmatic signifier": Freud's "death drive" is not a positive concept with a specific content, but a mere promise of some unspecified knowledge, the designation of a seductive mystery, of an entity which seems to account for the phenomena to be explained, although no one knows what it exactly means.

Is Lacan effectively guilty here? Is it not that the operation of the "enigmatic signifier" as described by Lear is the very operation of the Master-Signifier, of the universality and its constitutive exception? Lacan is not only aware of the trap of "substantializing" the rupture into a Beyond—he elaborated the "feminine" logic of the Non-All precisely in order to counter this logic of the universality and its exception. To put it succinctly, what Lear calls "break" is the space of what Lacan calls the act, the rupture in the symbolic narrative continuum, the "possibility of new possibilities," as Lear puts it, and the elementary "masculine" operation is precisely that of obliterating this dimension of the act. Crucial is here Lear's delineation of Freud's break with the Aristotelian ethics. Aristotle posits as the goal of life happiness—however, this is already a REFLECTED attitude (following Socrates), since in a pre-philosophical immersion into one's life-world, the question about the meaning and/or the goal of life "as such," in its entirety, cannot emerge. Which means that, in order to answer this question, to deal with life as a Whole, one has to introduce an exception, an element which no longer fits "normal" life—in Aristotle, this, of course, is pure Theory as the supreme self-satisfying activity, which, however, is ultimately inaccessible to us, mortals, since only God can practice it. At the very moment when the philosopher merely tries to conceive what would it mean to live a happy life, he thereby generates a foreign excess on account of which life can no longer be contained in itself...What Lear (re)discovers here in his own terms is Lacan's paradoxical logic of non-All: every totalization has to rely on an empty Master-Signifier which marks its constitutive exception. Consequently, does Lacan's logic of non-All not provide the very formula of what Lear calls "living with a remainder," abandoning the effort to contain the remainder by attaching it to a Master-Signifier and thus "re-substantializing" it, accepting that we dwell within a field that cannot ever be totalized?

Life thus loses its tautological self-satisfactory evidence: it comprises an excess which disturbs its balanced run. What does this mean? The premise of the theory of risk society and global reflexivization is that, today, one can be "addicted" to anything—not only to alcohol or drugs, but also to food, smoking, sex, work...This universalization of addiction points towards the radical uncertainty of any subjective position today: there are no firm predetermined patterns, everything has to be again and again (re)negotiated. And this goes up to suicide. Albert Camus, in his otherwise hopelessly outdated *The Myth of Sisyphus*, is right to emphasize that suicide is the only real philosophical problem—however, WHEN does it become this? Only in the modern reflexive society, when life itself no longer "goes by itself," as a "nonmarked" feature (to use this term developed by Roman Jakobson), but is "marked," has to be especially motivated (which is why euthanasia is becoming acceptable). Prior to modernity, suicide was simply a sign of some pathological malfunction, despair, misery. With reflexivization, however, suicide becomes an existential act, the outcome of a pure decision, irreducible to objective suffering or psychic pathology. This is the other side of Emile Durkheim's reduction of suicide to a social fact that can be quantified and predicted: the two moves, the objectivization/quantification of suicide and its transformation into a pure existential act, are strictly correlative. So, in short, what this loss of the spontaneous propensity to live means is that life itself becomes an object of addiction,[16] marked/stained by an excess, containing a "remainder" which no longer fits the simple life process. "To live" no longer means simply to pursue the balanced process of reproduction, but to get "passionately attached" or stuck to some excess, to some kernel of the Real, whose role is contradictory: it introduces the aspect of fixity or "fixation" into the life process—man is ultimately an animal whose life is derailed through the excessive fixation to some traumatic Thing.

In one of his (unpublished) seminars, Jacques-Alain Miller comments on an uncanny laboratory experiment with rats: in a labyrinthine setup, a desired object (a piece of good food or a sexual partner) is first made easily accessible to a rat; then, the setup is changed in such a way that the rat sees and thereby knows where the desired object is, but cannot gain access to it; in exchange for it, as a kind of consolation prize, a series of similar objects of inferior value is made easily accessible—how does the rat react to it? For some time, it tries to find its way to the "true" object; then, upon ascertaining that this object is definitely out of reach, the rat will renounce it and put up with some of the inferior substitute objects—in short, it will act as a "rational" subject of utilitarianism. It is only now, however, that the true experiment begins: the scientists performed a surgical operation on the rat, messing about with its brain, doing things to it with laser beams about which, as Miller put it delicately, it is better to know nothing. So what happened when the operated rat was again let loose in the labyrinth, the one in which the "true" object is inaccessible? The rat insisted: it never became fully reconciled with the loss of the "true" object and resigned itself to one of the inferior substitutes, but repeatedly returned to it, attempted to reach it. In short, the rat in a sense was humanized, it assumed the tragic "human" relationship towards the unattainable absolute object which, on account of its very inaccessibility, forever captivates our desire. (Miller's point, of course, is that this quasi-humanization of the rat resulted from its biological mutilation: the unfortunate rat started to act like a human being in relationship to its object of desire when its brain was butchered and crippled by means of an "unnatural" surgical intervention.) On the other hand, it is this very "conservative" fixation that pushes man to continuing renovation, since he never can fully integrate this excess into his life process. So we can see why did Freud use the term "death drive": the lesson of psychoanalysis is that humans are not simply alive, but possessed by a strange drive to enjoy life in excess of the ordinary run of things—and "death" stands simply and precisely for the dimension beyond "ordinary" biological life.

Human life is never "just life," it is always sustained by an excess of life which, phenomenally, appears as the paradoxical wound that makes us "undead," that prevents us to die (apart from Tristan's and Amfortas's wound in Wagner's *Tristan* and *Parsifal*, the ultimate figure of this wound is found in Kafka's "The Country Doctor"): when this wound is healed, the hero can die in peace. On the other hand, as Jonathan Lear is right to emphasize, the figures of the Ideal Life above the daily routine of life (like the Aristotelian contemplation) are all implicit stands-in for death: the only way to directly get at the excess of life is, again, to die. The basic

Christian insight is to combine these two opposite aspects of the same paradox: getting rid of the wound, healing it, is ultimately the same as fully and directly identifying with it—this is the ambiguity inscribed into the figure of Christ. He stands for the excess of life, for the "undead" surplus which persists over the cycle of generation and corruption: "I am come that they might have life, and that they might have it more abundantly." (St John 10:10) However, does his sacrifice simultaneously not stand for the obliteration of this excess? The story of (Adam's) Fall is evidently the story of how the human animal contracted the excess of Life which makes him/her human—"Paradise" is the name for the life delivered of the burden of this disturbing excess. Out of love for humanity, Christ then freely assumes, contract onto himself, the excess ("Sin") which burdened the human race.

Was, then, Nietzsche right in his claim that Christ was the only true Christian? By taking upon himself all the Sins and then, through his death, paying for them, Christ opens up the space for the redeemed humanity—however, by his death, people are not directly redeemed, but given the POSSIBILITY of redemption, of getting rid of the excess. This distinction is crucial: Christ does NOT do our work for us, he does not pay our debt, he "merely" GIVES US A CHANCE—with his death, he asserts OUR freedom and responsibility, i.e., he "merely" opens up the possibility, for us, to redeem ourselves through the "leap into faith," i.e., by way of choosing to "live in Christ"—*in imitatio Christi*, we REPEAT Christ's gesture of freely assuming the excess of Life, instead of projecting/displacing it onto some figure of the Other. (We put "merely" in quotation marks, since, as it was clear already to Kierkegaard, the definition of freedom is that possibility is higher than actuality: by giving us a chance to redeem ourselves, Christ does infinitely more than if he were directly to redeem ourselves.)

1. Deleuze, Gilles, *L'image-mouvement*, Paris: Éditions de Minuit, 1983, p. 234-236.
2. I borrowed this notion from Alenka Zupancic.
3. Wolf, Christa, *The Quest for Christa T.*, New York: Farrar, Straus & Giroux, 1970, p. 24.
4. Heidegger, Martin, *Zollikoner Seminare*, p. 260.
5. For a more detailed elaboration of this key feature, see Chapter 1 of Slavoj Zizek, *Did Somebody Say Totalitarianism?*, London: Verso, 2001, where I rely on Jean Laplanche's exemplary account in his *Essays on Otherness*, London: Routledge, 1999.
6. I am borrowing this formula of love as the "accessible transcendence" from Alenka Zupancic, to whom this whole passage is deeply indebted.
7. Kafka, Franz, *Wedding Preparations in the Country and Other Stories*, Harmondsworth: Penguin, 1978, p. 173-74.
8. Baas, Bernard, *De la Chose a l'objet*, Leuven: Pieters, 1998, especially p. 71-78.
9. Lacan, Jacques, *Écrits*, Paris: Seuil, 1966, p. 818.
10. These speculations of Lacan are clearly indebted to his friend Maurice Merleau-Ponty's explorations, posthumously collected in *Le visible et l'invisible*, Paris: Gallimard, 1964. Lacan refers to Merleau-Ponty especially in Part II of his *Four Fundamental Concepts of Psycho-Analysis*, New York: Norton, 1979.
11. Santner, Eric, "Epilogue," in *On the Psychotheology of Everyday Life*, Chicago: University of Chicago, 2001.
12. Bass, B., *Le désir pur*, Leuven: Peeters, 1992.
13. Lacan, J., *Le séminaire, Livre VII: L'éthique de la psychanalyse*, Paris: Seuil, 1986, p. 133.
14. See, for example, Jacques Lacan, "Desire and the interpretation of desire in Hamlet," in *Literature and Psychoanalysis*, ed. by Shoshana Felman, Baltimore: Johns Hopkins University, 1980, p. 15.
15. Lear, Jonathan, *Happiness, Death, and the Remainder of Life*, Cambridge: Harvard University, 2000.
16. For this idea, see Eric Santner's outstanding *On the Psychotheology of Everyday Life*.

# Rosemarie Trockel

## Josefina Ayerza

The wicked witch appeared and warned the princess dear, 'beware the rose, for when it pricks, you'll sleep a hundred year.' 'The evil spell,' a fairy cried, 'just might not have to be! A handsome prince—if brave and true—can kiss and set you free.'

Rosemarie Trockel's *Sleeping Beauty* right away raises the case as to esthetical parities concerning the famous fairy tale's belated images. Again, what other referent is there than the signifier provided you take on its meaning? Now you look quietly into the image, the questions crowding, but a head...swollen, asleep, dead...dying? And is it at all the head of a woman? Chances are your reflection upon the image won't fit the formal truth. And what this attests to is that Sleeping Beauty is not a signifier, but a name, indeed a spectre. The meaning it brings forth sets up the real. Legacy, or the surplus substracted from the legend, lurks in the spectre. When it verges on delusion it is because the name's place is void, kept void, celebrated as void. A rigid designator, it ascribes to the unmovable, it is not displaceable. Say you proclaim the Sleeping Beauty is a Mafioso, a passed out bum, a dead corpse, he will still be Sleeping Beauty however you describe him. Again, the singular topic, forever split between a story and a void, is not designated to reach its object. Its deeds lining up with melodrama, you recognize reality in fictional texts because that's where you come from.

ROSEMARIE TROCKEL, *Sleeping Beauty*, colored pencil on paper, 2000

There was one oddball, yet the many look-alikes. A pale fellow crested with a profusion of dark, wavy hair—you surmise his complexion is almost white by virtue of rice powder; that his lips, not necessarily colored, are nevertheless painted; that his eyes and eyebrows, emphasized with kohl and mascara, hide things...that the nose, too perfect, is fictitious, and also the ears— and he could be suffering though he's also smiling, vacillatingly, as if it all were a joke. A distraught audience has fingered him as  multiple, claimed that he may not have been him—the One—whatever it takes to make him an Other getting only worse. Again you surmise, joyful music, glittering candelabra, luxurious costumes, charisma, diamonds and dazzle...the Persian Room in New York's Plaza Hotel, the honky-tonk pianist in the movie *South Sea Sinner* with Shelley Winters, the Madison Square Garden, the Radio City Music Hall...and since Mr. Showmanship has no particular history, the figure in the portrait, thus the argument goes, must be Wladziu (Polish for Walter) Valentino Liberace. And it also is the many Liberaces—his famous chauffeurs—following Liberace's will to reproduce himself, outside himself, in other people's flesh, identical. The nature and dynamics of the operation are the domain of the character's myth, which also tells you how Liberace, a maverick of cloning, used human beings to extract himself from others, to be in the Other flesh. Trockel's drawing retains the label *Untitled* on behalf of profusive metonymy, or the many speculations...not so much from the One over to an Other, but from the Other over to the One.

ROSEMARIE TROCKEL, *Untitled*, photocopy on paper. 1993

An asleep, inert baby, a target mark over his chest...*The Misfortune*. A 1991 interview with Meyer Vaisman comes to mind; on the occasion Vaisman told of the popular festivals in his native country. Thus, in Venezuela, when a baby dies they proceed to boil him, and then they dress him in white and paint him as an angel. In addition the baby gets paper wings and is then set on a table. With people dancing and feasting, around the table the infant represents a newcomer in heaven. When the party concludes they hang the baby on a hook over the front door, so everybody can see that there is a new name in heaven. Angels, said Vaisman, are always children... Thus ensued the different sort of angels in my mind, specially the ones consisting of a head and a pair of wings, those that have certainly being equated to signifiers, and yes, they fly. With Trockel the names in heaven mark the body of the baby by cutting around the heart. And the invisible sitgmata is resolved only when the desperate search for meaning yields to the agency of the signifier—whose misfortune is it?

An inert *Young Man Dozing*, it was past twelve o'clock when he awoke. The sun flowing in through the curtains of the room, rays of light bathed his face, arms, and torso. In the dream he was a butterfly. Now he says to himself—it's only a dream. Again, still pondering over the fancy, he comes to ask himself whether it is the butterfly who dreams he—the butterfly—is Choang-tsu...

ROSEMARIE TROCKEL, *Le malheur (The Misfortune)*, colored pencil on board, 2000

He is not mad, first because Choang-tsu doesn't regard himself as absolutely identical with Choang-tsu, and secondly because he does not fully understand how right he is. Why is he so right? According to Jacques Lacan when he was the butterfly that he apprehended one of the roots of his identity—that he was and is, in his essence that butterfly who paints himself with his own colors—and it is because of this that, in the last resort, he is Choang-tsu. Because of the nature of dreams it's not likely that while he is the butterfly he would start wondering whether, when he is Choang-tsu awake, he is not the butterfly he is dreaming of being. Now he dreams of being the butterfly, now he wakes up and wants to tell the story. Not that he represented himself as a butterfly, he was a butterfly. This does not mean he is bewitched by the butterfly—he is a witch butterfly, yet spelled by no one, for in the dream he is a butterfly for nobody. It is when he is awake that he is Choang-tsu for others—entrapped in their butterfly net.

ROSEMARIE TROCKEL, *Young Man Dozing*, pencil on paper, 2000

# Intercepts

GERMÁN GARCÍA. Buenos Aires

FREUD AND THE CHILD WOMAN

To talk of a child woman is a pleonasm, because in each woman you are looking for a girl: a forever infant consecrated by the Napoleon Code. Yet, if in a woman you look for a girl, what do you look for in a woman? Sigmund Freud got to know it while reflecting on the eventuality of a love triangle. The mise-en-scene, about to take place in the Vienna cafes well before the city is transfigured by the rise of Nazism, the protagonists in the triangle are Fritz Wittels (the Viennese doctor who in 1905 was part of Freud's circle and editor of the magazine *Die Fackel*), Karl Kraus (famous satiric writer and editor of the same magazine) and a young woman. The seventeen years old Irma Karczewska, Kraus' invention of an ac-

RINEKE DIJKSTRA, still from video *The Buzzclub, Liverpool, UK/Mysterywold, Zaandam, NL*, 1996-1998

tress to fill in after the death of Annie Kalmar, the German actress who had been his first love. The triangle between Wittels, Kraus and Karczewska becomes the centerpiece of *Freud and the Child Woman*.[1]

WHY IS FRITZ WITTELS IGNORED?

When in March 1932, the New York Psychoanalytic Association acknowledged the endorsement bestowed upon Wittels by the Vienna division, the Austrian doctor was already loaded with a mischievous itinerary that had compelled him to emigrate to the New World with his family. Although Wittels came to America carrying with him a biography of Freud (the one he wrote in 1924)[2] he was already parting ways with Freud's inner circle: he had undergone analysis with William Steckel—who Freud dubbed "pig" in various languages.[3] By then, Freud had also broken up with Karl Kraus, a dangerous opponent, with whom he used to entertain a distant yet peaceful relation. Up to 1910 Wittels "ambivalence" accounted for him collaborating in Kraus' magazine, while advancing to Freud and his followers a diagnosis of the neurotic incitements of *Die Fackel*'s chief-editor.

Freud writes to Ferenczi, and this is a rather daring conjecture, what he deems to be Kraus' innermost: "He is a mediocre fool endowed with an histrionic talent." Wittels, in 1910, goes on to publish a novel to praise Irma the "child woman," and thus answer Kraus' aphoristic attacks against psychoanalysis and his own person. The friendship shattered, Kraus, who once credited him as the supreme writer of the German tongue, was now saying that Wittels looked good only because of his plagiarizing him.

Now Freud tries to deter the novel *Ezequiel der Zugereiste* from being published. He tells Wittels, "I will be brief: if you don't publish the book you won't lose a thing, but if you do publish it you will lose everything." Wittels gave up Freud's circle and published the novel. Kraus took the matter to court—not Freud's group that was against the scandal and the scandalous one. So Wittels is dimly known, even though he made a career in psychoanalysis, having an early stand on abortion, women's rights and sexual freedom.

IRMA LA DOUCE

By 1907 Kraus and Wittels had become close friends, they shared nights in cafes, they both wrote in *Die Fackel*. So Wittels neglects his career as a medical doctor, and his psychoanalytic practice. In 1908 Wittels' father dies, the fact providing for a closer approach to Freud and a progressive distance from Kraus, it will end in the 1910 sundering. Soon he will break up with Freud. Wittels remains alone. Freud's letters though—in the memoirs edited by Edward Timms—show how fonder of the misguided disciple he was, than the official version let's you know.

By then Kraus had entered into a controversy with the editors of *Die Strunde*, given to search in his private life so as to attack him. Between these journalists a certain Samuel Wilder stood out, later on to become a famous Hollywood director under the name of Billy Wilder (Edward Timms asks himself if it was on this occasion that Wilder discovered the story of the naive prostitute, which he would later film with the title of *Irma la Douce*). *Die Stunde* was an occasional enemy, since Kraus' constant struggle was against the paper *Neue Freie Presse*, insofar as it had great influence on artist's destinies by way of its compliments or its rejections. Edward Hanslich was knocking Wagner over and Marx Nordau was trying to destroy Ibsen, Nietsche, Tolstoi and Zolz. Moritz Benedikt (director of the *Neue Freise Presse*) entertained long editorials in the financial and political sections to "the reactionary turned into liberals through convenience, besides writing a weekly column on the stock market." For the reading public of the time the parallel version of these enraged pieces and the none less enraged parodies, critics and acuteness of *Die Fackel*, was a feast, the director often to mingle in the antagonist paper through camouflaging letters to the editor with a pseudonym.

Though none of this was of interest for Irma Karczewska,

too busy with fitting Annie Kalmar's place, "promiscuous, passionate, joyous, unprejudiced, drunken and intelligent without being cultivate," according to Wittels description of her. Yet earlier, in 1907, he pictures Kraus favorite creation in a vibrant article called "The Child Woman." He published in *Die Fackel* in these terms: "The young woman in question has a great sex appeal, developed so early that she is forced to initiate her sexual life when she is still a child in other aspects. Along her whole sexual life she continues to be a hypersexual child, without being able to understand the civilized world of adults." He would also garnish her with allusions to Helen of Troy, Lucrecia Borgia, Manon Lescaut and the Nana of Zola. Irma wouldn't understand and was not in the least interested in the Byzantine compliments; she was happy enough knowing these inclinations inscribed her in that gallery of names.

Some time before the breakup, in one of the Wednesday meetings at Freud's Circle, Wittels read his work where he concluded this child girl was serene, her sensuality without lust, since she was a creature free of neurosis. Freud, rather discomforted, answered that she was ragged (*Haderlump*) and added that it wasn't the intention of psychoanalysis to create wildness, but to help in the getting to know, and the control of sexuality. Irma had failed to pass the examination. The same way that little K was not Freud's taste; he preferred modesty and mistrusted feminine liberality.

In a journey to Venice (by then a kind of colony of Vienna) Irma displayed her caprices. The city Kraus and Wittels would identify to Casanova, Byron and Shakespeare, was a bore for the daughter of a doorman. At the beach, instead of looking at the sea she would be trying to seduce Siegfried Wagner—son of Richard—who in turn was seducing Isadora Duncan. She couldn't care less about Tiziano, Bellini and Veronese; instead she cared for the minimal parts of a huge statue of Hercules. She demanded from Kraus a mahogany piano and she made the kind of scandals that Gombrowicz's schoolgirl and Nobokov's Lolita would have applauded.

After the disaster of the excursion, the two Viennese cavaliers tried to get the famous actor Alexander Giraldi to recommend her to a great Berlin director, called Kren. Irma was an awful actress, she had an impossible voice, still she got the appointment. Kraus had invented her a past life, the same way he wanted to invent for her a future. He was responsible for having detached her from her environment and for making her compete with the rich whores of central Vienna. Wittels writes, "Kraus still pretended to be in ecstasy because of the girl's divine beauty, but the truth is he didn't stand her gibberish and so introduced her to more and more men, so that they would take her away, for them to distract her." Some time before the triangle's definite breakup, confirmed through the 1910 scandal, Kraus told Wittels a dream, this dream he considered a bad premonition: Benedikt, his very bad enemy, the director of *Neue Freie Presse*, was greeted with a reverence by Fritz Wittels. Very soon, Kraus convinced Irma to refuse Wittels' marriage proposal, and redoubled the attacks against his ex-companion throughout philosophical aphorisms. Thus continuing with his projects, he married Irma to an Austrian industrialist. After the Great War, she would remarry a certain Hal Triadou, who died in 1926. Frank Wedekind also cultivated the Woman Child myth (he displays his version called Lulu in two of his literary works).

WHERE IS MY FATHER?

Wittels use to say that Kraus was his literary father and that Freud was his analytical father (even though his patient was the architect Adolf Loos). However he also had a biological father who died in 1908, when he was still in his twenties: "The boy we carry inside asks in anguish: where is my father? and he looks for him in all those people clothed with authority. So I went to see Freud and told him my father was dead, Freud answered: 'we will continue to work together and we will work together.'" Wittels writes then *Sexuelle Not*. He dedicates it to Freud, who tells him Kraus would take vengeance for that. In fact Kraus writes: "Psychoanalysis is the sickness for what this media pretends to be the cure." The grace of the aphorism resides in the fact that the word "media" refers as much to *Die Fackel* as to psychoanalysis.

*Ezequiel der Zugereiste*, Wittels' novel, has a character called Benjamin Disgusting that publishes a magazine called *Die Groß Nase* (it alludes to Kraus' big nose). The novel sold throughout various editions, it was a transparent *roman à clef* for those who wondered in and out of the bohemian cafes. It was easy for Kraus to win the lawsuit in defense of Irma's honor, who happy with her place as heroine told Wittels: "I told him that I was still in love with you, but he answered: What a bad taste!

What did Freud take from this mischievous story? There are various answers: 1) that the other's woman is of interest because the third one's prejudice can be a sexual condition; 2) that the mother comes to play when the case is a third one's redemption; 3) that the woman child, in her corporeal ambiguity satisfies masculine and feminine tendencies; 4) that ambivalence is the difficulty deciding between desire and the ideal; 5) that beautiful women, criminals, and wild animals fascinate our narcissism; 6) that the USA offers a way out to those who don't resolve these problems.

As for Wittels, after immigrating to America he lived on giving conferences, an fellow researcher at the Bellevue Hospital. An associate psychoanalyst at Columbia University, he finished in a peculiar position: as defender of the Freudian orthodoxy against the Ego Psychology of Heinz Hartman, and the feminist critique initiated by Karen Horney.

---

1. Wittels, Fritz, *Freud and the Child Woman: The Memoirs of Fritz Wittels*, Eduard Timms (Editor), New Haven: Yale University Press, 1996.
2. Wittels, F., *Sigmund Freud: His Personality, His teaching and His School*, NY: Grosset & Dunlap, 1950.
3. Freud used to address Stekel and Adler as Max and Moritz, the two cruel kids from Wilhem Buch's humorist story.

MIGUEL ABREU, New York

## THE BALLAD OF ION LUPESCU: OR 222 MINUTES TO LIVE*

> *In the beginning was the Word...* - John 1:1

> *...but there is also the notion of drive, of the blind compulsion to repeat which can never be sublated in the ideal medium of language.* - Slavoj Zizek

### 1. THE STORY

*The Ballad of Ion Lupescu* recounts the odyssey of a celebrated Romanian athlete sometime after the fall of the Ceausescu regime. In 1993, yielding to a long-awaited opportunity to try his luck in the New World, Ion Lupescu defected from his homeland and settled in an emerging suburb of Los Angeles. There, evidently feeling somewhat isolated at the edge of the Mojave desert, the track star and national hero spends his days training, running across the landscapes and traversing the many construction sites of the new city.

Following various, high-level diplomatic efforts to reestablish contact with the sprinter, a detective, an athlete himself and an ex-member of the *Securitate* forces has been sent to the region on a mission to find Lupescu and bring him home safely to Bucharest. The detective's only clue is a snapshot taken at the Pasadena Rose Bowl during the 1994 World Cup, in which the hero is seen mingling with a group of fans, standing behind the pierced flag of the Revolution.

Sitting back with his feet up on a desk located in what

---

\* A cut and paste essay about the video by Pieter Schoolwerth and Miguel Abreu.

resembles an outdoor TV game-show studio, the detective wonders how to begin his search. Suddenly, the phone rings: "I need you to want me," murmurs a voice with a Romanian accent; "without you I am lost, with nothing to believe in. I love you, find me," the man continues at the other end of the line. The bewildered investigator recognizes Lupescu, but the caller hangs up. With his portable phone in hand, the detective hurries and jots down the message word for word. What to make of this delirious declaration questions the special agent? He glances at the handset in a state of confusion, focuses on the dial plate and becomes intrigued by the ordinary fact that to each number on the dial corresponds a series of three letters, in alphabetical order. Scrutinizing further, he notices that no character appears above figure 1, and that on top of 0, the exceptional four-letter abbreviation, OPER, eludes the previous systematic arrangement. He also discovers that the letters Q and Z have been omitted from the alphabet altogether.

The detective reflects upon these findings for a moment and proceeds with the curious task of inscribing, under each character of the English language text, its corresponding digit on the dia. He adds up the resulting numbers and obtains 440. Could this figure amount to some sort of lead? After checking his watch, which reads 1 p.m. the detective prepares to leave and stuffs a few chosen items in his briefcase, including the phone, the calculator and indeed, the written message. He stands up, crosses the set and races away, with the firm intention of completing 440 strides directly straight ahead. What will our special agent discover at the end of his run? This entire operation will come to constitute the first leg of an unprecedented effort to track down Lupescu in and out of suburbia.

*What do individualism or social conquests imply when it comes to the need for images? What does an individual expect from images that, unlike the images of advertising, would not exist to hide other images, but would open up onto something else?*

## 2. THE GENERATORS OF THE IMAGE

Glimpsing at the seemingly endless billboards that flank the longest boulevards in the world, walking through the huge shopping malls that make up the heart of Southern Californian cities, the ubiquitous presence in space of the three primary colors soon becomes natural to the eye. Blue, yellow and bright red spring up from almost everywhere, and in an infinite variety of ways these particular hues give shape to the horizon line. Thus, since outdoor documentary photography was to be our basic production mode, this immediate visual fact was to infiltrate our story and sway the images that would tell it.

Blue, yellow and red are also the three colors of the Romanian flag, and it so happened that this nation's soccer team had qualified for the 1994 World Cup held in the United States. So in order to encourage our protagonists to feel at ease and move freely in the environment they would inhabit, it seemed appropriate for them to have roots in that far away country.

Ion Lupescu was and perhaps still is a professional sprinter. It will therefore come as no surprise that to run—and to sprint—remain dominant activities for our hero. But he has also become a clever, if not shrewd user of the telephone system. In fact, the narrative as a whole is deeply permeated by telecommunications riddles. Does not the detective's search actually make ground through repeated efforts to decode increasingly mysterious phone messages? And since, remarkably, one of the major American telecommunications operators is called 'Sprint,' and because that company's logo is solidly anchored in our common media space, it simply fitted the present order of things to risk diverting this glaring confluence of meaning into our own, integrated plan to generate fiction.

## 3. The Structuring Elements of Time and Space

If an overt color scheme pervades the production design and sustains the composition of each frame, the time and space articulated in the video, for their part, are the direct outgrowth of Lupescu's incantations. Translated into numbers corresponding to specific distances to be traveled, these same love messages will further impose time constraints the detective will need to comply with in the hope to fulfill his mission.

Thus the uttered word, here, functions as the ultimate principle of organization, the blind law which, after being tamed and interpreted, will inspire the frenzy of a breathtaking manhunt. And as the viewer will soon observe from a higher perspective, the simultaneous outcome of this very physical chase will resemble nothing but a drawing of discrete geometrical shapes upon the wonderland of suburbia. The delineated blue triangle, yellow square and red pentagon, all expanding from a shared center, will fix the contours of closed worlds in which quasi-secret indigenous languages oversee separate states of affairs.

Ion Lupescu himself would probably feel compelled to live out his apparent lunacy, his sense of perdition even more, should he not be somehow conscious that a concerted effort to find him is positively underway. And while our two heroes are being drawn into a high stake game that is quickly turning into a matter of life and death, they are also progressively sliding into becoming one and the same.

Strictly speaking, however, the stakes for our prey are to maintain a delicate balance between continuing to tease the detective into everlasting action and managing to retain the slight lead he needs on his tireless pursuer. One might even consider that the fragile distance separating the two sides, the two incarnations of our double protagonist, operates as the space of desire itself, the minimum gap necessary for projection to occur, the interval without which things would become dangerously equal to themselves, that is to say non-existent.

*Advertising...has made us accustomed to seeing only one character, one body at the time. What they sold, were it deodorant or Marlboros, didn't matter at all. What mattered was to see a single individual in a non-environment: a bit of blue sky, a swimming-pool...The question of re-building the environment is crucial, since we don't know the world the modern individual will live in.*

*It comes down to editing: the word images is often used, but they are no more. The one thing remaining is relations. Americans, who are more pragmatic, make use of that force.*

*An image is never alone, it always calls for another. But today, what are called images are ensembles of solitude connected by something being said...*

*...Movies are not one image after another, they are one image plus another, which forms a third image. This third one is formed by the spectator the moment he sees. The film is an image that becomes more and more precise, like the work of the musician or the painter.*

### 4. TOPOGRAPHY OF A PHANTOM CITY

One of the primary intentions fueling the project was to always remain receptive to the environment underlying the story. We were to linger on the territory's surfaces hoping to grasp the effects of its dreams before imagining the characters' psychological make-up and devising the staging of their relationships. The aim was to also render palpable the rationalization of time and space governing the development of our city refuge, ode to the consumer king, to private property and to the seclusion of life. This safe and rapidly growing suburb, built from scratch by adding one master-planned housing complex to another, attracts new home owners everyday by offering a variety of residential styles, ranging from the luxurious Mediterranean villa for the more prosperous citizens all the way to the pseudo-English cottage on a hill geared to the lower income prospects. Here we stood at the crossroads of the empire of the sign, where straight lines and right angles reign supreme, and where private security cars patrol to enforce the established distances between places and between people. And as we glided along the glorious road network servicing the area, we noticed that the basic act of walking had become limited to the mall, the new replacement town center where, as if by miracle, a semblance of social life still seemed possible.

Against this background, confronting the general feeling of solitude overtaking the city, the telephones ring, ring and ring again, runners and sports practitioners are everywhere, and the TV sets of the region stay on 24 hours a day.

*...man has been violently thrown out of himself, on the surface of things he can neither digest nor refuse. Things are "there" because of him, but outside of him forever, without reason, in a sudden and inexplicable state of upsurge.*
*Genuine communication is a projection outside oneself; not an act of pouring out, but a physical—metaphysical—identification which, far from absorbing it, leaves undiminished the other's freedom. Sometimes, when one fixes that point (an object, a person), one actually becomes that point; and it is the movement of that passage to the other that matters.*

5. THE SPECTER OF MULTIPLE APPEARANCES

If at first sight the *The Ballad of Ion Lupescu* resembles a detective story, the viewer will soon recognize the call of various other genres without being able to decide to which alternative option the narrative best belongs. Apprehended from this particular angle, the film will remain unresolved as it fails to identify convincingly with the rules of any given genre.

Are we watching the unfolding of a kind of burlesque thriller, or is what we are witnessing closer to a commercial prolonging itself to the point of turning into a modern-day tragedy? And as to the central set, is it acceptable as a detective's office, or does it function more like a TV game-show studio a la "Wheel of Fortune"? For the increasingly discerning spectator, however, apart from the 'no comment' documentary depiction of the region, several more cryptic associations might offer clues to a more fundamental reading : Is Ion Lupescu, standing on top of a podium with his arms raised to the sky, reminiscent of Moses on the sacred mountain receiving the Ten Commandments? Or in the end, does not the very design of the enacted chase bring to mind the structure of a mandala? And is not this latter correlation facilitated by the recurring view of the circular set seen from above, as well as by the less obvious fact that mandalas, following Dr. Jung's psychological description, "appear spontaneously in dreams, in certain states of conflict, and in cases of schizophrenia"? Are not the hero's actions and reactions the consequence of these precise states of mind? By contrast, for a dedicated psychoanalyst of the Lacanian school of thought, the project would probably be more fruitfully examined from the perspective of a case study on perverse behavior. Indeed, as Slavoj Zizek has noted recently, pertaining to the pervert - and perhaps also to Lupescu - "since for him the Law is not fully established (the Law is his *lost* object of desire), he supplements this lack with an intricate set of *regulations* (the masochistic ritual). The crucial point is, therefore, to bear in mind the opposition between Law and regulations (or 'rules'): the latter bear witness to the absence or suspension of Law."

Be that as it may, let us not forget that from the onset our foremost concern has always been to stay in touch with the growing number of extreme sports aficionados and to reach out to the worldwide audience of MTV. And if by chance and in the same breath the video proves of interest to the student of Egyptology and the mere lover of drawing, we will consider it to have achieved its range of potential meaning.

### 6. Speedvision vs. the static images of the Ceausescu regime

One of the significant techno-cultural developments of the last decade has been the dramatic emergence of "data-processing". We, as human beings - our tastes, habits, physical attributes, levels of income and opinions of all sorts - are increasingly being considered as statistical evidence to be processed to make allegedly more and more efficient decisions about almost everything. This in part is a direct result of the so-called digital revolution which has been turning our living environment into a grand theater of numbers and signs, all the way to the internal structure of images themselves.

The effects of this far reaching evolution is the ultimate subject of *The Ballad of Ion Lupescu*. We set out to make the first film about "data-processing," literally with and through "data-processing." The basic bent of the story is that, as opposed to allowing external entities such as large corporations and government institutions to transpose our protagonist's features and dispositions into different kinds of data, Lupescu assertively invents his own private numbers and secret codes and makes resolutely independent calculations that will produce the very time and space of the video.

The other crucial theme fueling the work is the invading effect of advertising. We captured on camera the unavoidable presence in space of signs and billboards and attempted to create a cinematic mode that would absorb some of the immense powers of commercials by re-channeling them into our singular, tragi-comic purposes. The strategy, if you will, was one of reverse product placement, in which a selected big name brand and its accompanying message is neutralized by connecting it to a recurring theme or action in the story—the most glaring example of this device being Lupescu's sprints surging out of the 'Sprint' telecommunications starting-blocks. And as the swirling world of TV ads and dancing signs begins to contaminate the documentary image of the film, an opposition emerges between what might be called the rapid and hollow 'informational image' on the one hand and the 'memory image' of the static Ceausescu regime on the other.

What Lupescu is feeling, in a sense, is the pressure of these two kinds, these two dominant modes of the image. What he is doing, in the end, is organizing his struggle to escape by inventing a secret order of the image, an order of resistance in the name of the documentary image.

NEW AND NOTEWORTHY BOOKS

by Richard G. Klein

Badiou, Alain
*Ethics, An Essay on the Understanding of Evil*
New York: Verso, 2001.
Badiou, Alain
*Manifesto for Philosophy*
Albany: SUNY Press, 1999.
Barcilai, Shuli
*Lacan and the Matter of Origins*
Stanford: Stanford University Press, 1999.
Butler, Judith and Laclau, Ernesto and Zizek, Slavoj
*Contingency, Hegemony, Universality*
New York: Verso, 2000.
Houis, Jacques and Mieli, Paola and Stafford, Marc
*Being Human The Technological Extensions of the Body*
New York: Agincourt/Marsilio, 1999.
Lacan, Jacques
*Écrits*
new complete translation by Bruce Fink
New York: Norton, 2001.
Lacan, Jacques
*TheSeminar, Book IV: The Object Relation*
New York: Norton, 2001.
Lacan, Jacques
*TheSeminar, Book XVII: The Other Side of Psychoanalysis*
translated by Russell Grigg
New York: Norton, 2001.
MacCannell, Juliet Flower
*The Hysteric's Guide to the Future Female*
St. Paul: University of Minnesota, 1999.
Malone, Kareen Ror and Stephen Friedlander
*The Subject Of Lacan, A Lacanian Reader for Psychologists*
Albany: SUNY Press, 2000.
Muller, John and Brent, Joseph
*Peirce, Semiotics, and Psychoanalysis*
Baltimore: Johns Hopkins University Press, 2000.

NOBUS, DANY
*Jacques Lacan and the Freudian Practice of Psychoanalysis*
New York: Routledge, 2000.

PSYCHONALYTICAL NOTEBOOK OF THE LONDON CIRCLE
*Issue 5, January 2001, Fantasy and Castration*
European School of Psychoanalysis. josessions@aol.com

RAGLAND, ELLIE and METZGER, DAVID
*Logical Sexuation—Aristotle to Lacan*
New York: Routledge, 2000.

KALPANA SESHADRI-CROOKS
*Desiring Whiteness - A Lacanian analysis of race*
New York: Routledge, 2000.

SHEPHERDSON, CHARLES
*Vital Signs: Nature, Culture, Psychoanalysis*
New York: Routledge, 2000.

STAVRAKAKIS, YANNIS
*Lacan and the Political*
New York: Routledge, 2000.

VAN PELT, TAMISE
*The Other Side of Desire; Lacan's Theory of the Registers*
Albany: SUNY Press, 2000.

ZIZEK, SLAVOJ
*The Ticklish Subject*
New York: Verso, 1999.

ZIZEK, SLAVOJ
*The Fragile Absolute, Or Why the Christian Legacy is Worth Fighting For*
New York: Verso, 2000.

ZIZEK SLAVOJ
*Did Somebody Say Totalitarism? Five Essays in the (Mis)Use Of A Notion*
New York: Verso, 2001.

ZIZEK SLAVOJ
*The Fright of Real Tears, Kieslowski and The Future*
Bloomington: Indiana University Press. 2001

ZIZEK SLAVOJ
*Enjoy Your Symptom! Jacques Lacan In Hollywood and Out*
second expanded edition, New York: Routledge 2000.

ZUPANCIC, ALENKA
*Ethics of the Real: Kant, Lacan*
New York: Verso, 2000.

# PSYCHOANALYTICAL NOTEBOOKS
## A biannual publication of the London Circle of
## the European School of Psychoanalysis

| PN 1: *SYMPTOM* | PN 2: *THE UNCONSCIOUS* |
|---|---|

**PN 3: *LOVE***

| | |
|---|---|
| Jacques-Alain Miller | *Of Semblants in the Relation Between Sexes* |
| Patricia Johansson-Rosen | *Of a Love that would be the Semblant* |
| Rose-Paule Vinciguerra | *The Paradoxes of Love* |
| Antonio Di Ciaccia | *The Love of God and of the Neighbour* |
| Rachel Fajersztajn | *'I Love to You'* |
| Bogdan Wolf | *From the Signifier to Love* |
| Véronique Voruz | *The Scene by the Lake: When Desire Fails as Defence* |
| Adrian Price | *Jealousy as a Mechanism of Defence in the case of Dora* |
| Jacques-Alain Miller | *The Disparate* |
| Marie De Souza | *From the Subject of Science to the Subject of the Unconscious* |
| Natalie Charraud | *Cantor with Lacan (1)* |
| Richard Klein | *Responsibility in Psychoanalysis* |
| Pierre-Gilles Gueguen | *The Pass Between Knowledge and Belief* |
| Vincent Dachy | *Do not Confuse the Real(s)* |
| Marie-Hélène Brousse | *Sexual Position and the End of Analysis* |

**PN 4: *PSYCHIATRY AND PSYCHOANALYSIS***

| | |
|---|---|
| Jacques Lacan | *British Psychiatry and the War* |
| Eric Laurent | *The Real and the Group* |
| Philip Dravers | *Making-do with* jouissance |
| Jacques-Alain Miller | *Contraindications to Psychoanalytical Treatment* |
| Serge Cottet | *Four Preliminary Questions to a Renewal of the Clinic* |
| François Sauvagnat | *On the Specificity of Elementary Phenomena* |
| Jean-Claude Maleval | *Why so many 'Borderlines'?* |
| Vicente Palomera | *An Error in Diagnosis: Causes and Consequences* |
| Bernard Porcheret | *Hands off my Symptom* |
| Jean-Pierre Deffieux | *The Use of Metonymy in a Case of Psychosis* |
| Roger Litten | *Transference and Demand in Psychosis* |
| Nathalie Charraud | *Cantor with Lacan (2)* |
| Richard Klein | *Technique and Ethics in Psychoanalysis* |

**PN 5: *FANTASY AND CASTRATION***

To appear in January 2001. Contributors include:
Jacques-Alain Miller, Eric Laurent, Pierre Naveau, Pierre Skriabine, Catherine Bonningue, Jean-Luc Monnier, Bogdan Wolf, Sophie Marret, Penny Georgiou.

## TO SUBSCRIBE send your order to:
## LCESPNotebooks@aol.com

Prices for 2 issues (incl. p&p)-UK: £18.00, Europe: £20.00, Outside Europe: £24.00. Payment by cheque (UK and France), credit card (2 issues only, the payment to be drawn by Rathbone Books), or transfer.

Credit card _____ No _____-_____-_____-_____
Name _____ Address _____
_____ Country_____
Issues to subscribe to: ☐No1 ☐No2 ☐No3 ☐No4 ☐No5 ☐No6 ☐No7
London Circle of the ESP, 17b Granville Road, London N4 4EJ
www.londoncircle-esp.com

www.lacan.com

acan dot com is jacques lacan in the US

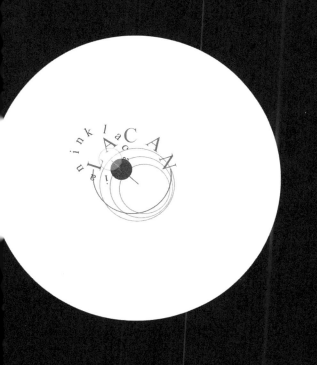

# SUBSCRIBE TO *lacanian ink*

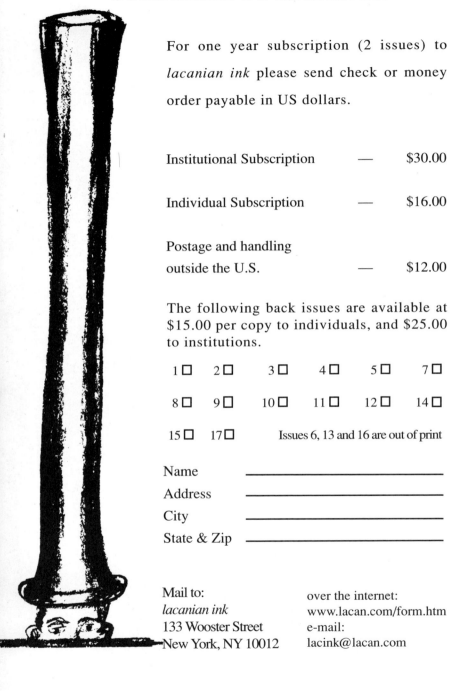

For one year subscription (2 issues) to *lacanian ink* please send check or money order payable in US dollars.

| | | |
|---|---|---|
| Institutional Subscription | — | $30.00 |
| Individual Subscription | — | $16.00 |
| Postage and handling outside the U.S. | — | $12.00 |

The following back issues are available at $15.00 per copy to individuals, and $25.00 to institutions.

1 ☐  2 ☐  3 ☐  4 ☐  5 ☐  7 ☐

8 ☐  9 ☐  10 ☐  11 ☐  12 ☐  14 ☐

15 ☐  17 ☐   Issues 6, 13 and 16 are out of print

Name  _____
Address  _____
City  _____
State & Zip  _____

Mail to:
*lacanian ink*
133 Wooster Street
New York, NY 10012

over the internet:
www.lacan.com/form.htm
e-mail:
lacink@lacan.com